What readers are saying:

It made me laugh many times, made me cry and left me with a good warm feeling and inspired. Really a good read!
--T.W. Santa Barbara, California

An unusual book here and one with appeal, depth, interest and I want to see the movie!!
--E.B. New York, N.Y.

And have said:

We have all said that you can write.
--James A. Michener

The Wrath of Grapes

How Not to Start a Winery

k.f. jones

Corvo Publication

Lockwood, California

PUBLISHED BY CORVO PUBLICATIONS
Post Office Box 89
Lockwood, CA 93932
www.volodelcorvo.com

Copyright © 2008 by k.f. jones

Manufactured in the United States of America

Publisher's Cataloging-in-Publication
(Provided by Quality Books, Inc.)

        Jones, K. F. (Kenneth Frederick)
        The wrath of grapes : how not to start a winery /
    K.F. Jones.
        p. cm.
        ISBN-13: 978-0-9701592-6-7
        ISBN-10: 0-9701592-6-9

        1. Jones, K. F. (Kenneth Frederick) 2. Vintners--
California--Biography. 3. Wine and wine making--
California. 4. Wine industry--California. I. Title.

TP547.J66A3 2008   641.2'2'092
                   QBI08-600013

Edited by Katy Meigs and John Raymond, Ojai, California

Printed by Thomson-Shore, Inc.

Acknowledgments

To the Angels and womanhood in general, a special vote of gratitude. Not that all Angels are women. Grandpa Bill and my stepfather, Ralph W. James, were and I am sure are. Not that all women are angels, but I will hold the door open for you anyway.

To the Demons, a class that is not gender exclusive. Just to let you know I am grateful for having lived very well. Very well.

Prologue

If you don't set goals, you can't regret not reaching them.
--Yogi Berra

The pitch came from high over the right shoulder. The sun, seemingly pulled from the heavens with the vengeance of a Nordic god, was destined for the center of my forehead. The university starter had needed some live batters, and I was among the coach's handpicked fodder, selected from a pool of freshmen wannabes. It was an unofficial workout and lacking in equipment, which notably also excluded batting helmets.

I had cracked the first offering--low and away, out of the strike zone--into short center field. A line-drive base hit in anybody's league. And for one brief moment I thought that maybe I could do this...every boy's dream: play college ball, and then maybe the majors? But on its way to short center field that line drive had come perilously close to the bill of Thor's cap. Lessons number one and two: freshman wannabes shouldn't show up senior starting pitchers that resemble Nordic gods, and then almost take his head off in the process.

Instead of the strike zone, the pitcher glared at a place where my third eye would have been. And if I'd had one, the delivery of the next pitch seemed destined to lend new meaning to the baseball bromide about keeping your eye on the ball. "Stand in there," I told myself. "It's a curve and it's gonna break." I waited until I had nearly gone cross-eyed before bailing out. It was not graceful, with self-preservation taking precedence over dignity. I crumpled into a pitiful heap and proceeded to dig a fallout shelter under home plate. I resurfaced in time to hear the pitcher query the coach, who was standing in as umpire behind the catcher, if that had been a strike. The coach nodded affirmatively.

As the dust settled, I realized that I had been grossly outclassed. If a ball could break that much so late...well, I was more in awe than embarrassed. Though there was plenty of justification for both.

This book is not about baseball, although I do believe that no true story that takes place in America during the last half of the twentieth century (and into the next) can be complete without it. This is a book about dreams and one particular dream and some that have been dashed, or gracefully released, and just a lot of dumb things that can happen in the pursuit of dreams. And here baseball serves to illustrate the latter admirably.

This is a book about starting a winery, and included herein is an account of lessons learned along the way about life...and death. If starting a winery is a dream of yours, and you are considering such a venture, or if you are determined absolutely not to ever do such an idiotic thing--wouldn't ever *dream* of it--there is support for your conviction within these pages either way. There are other dreams addressed here, both the day and night kind. But building a winery, albeit a very small one, is the central one and serves at least as a paradigm for following dreams.

If you are interested in making home wine, you will find assistance, support, and encouragement. If you just love wine, you will find fellowship and you might be interested in what goes on before you pull the cork out of the bottle. And your appreciation for what your favorite winemaker has accomplished could be multiplied tenfold. There are so many out there making some great wines. If you have just been introduced to the beverage, you are most welcome aboard.

My philosophy in one sentence: *Wine is learning what you like, not being taught what to like.* Finally, if you just like a good read, I have been told that I am a better writer than a winemaker or baseball player. But, then again, those who have said so were wine critics and baseball scouts. Above all, I hope the reader will have a few laughs. I like to make people laugh, and strive to do so frequently as a personal gift. I have heard it said that laughter adds eight years to one's life. The events recounted have probably taken a greater toll from mine.

Giving up the baseball dream was not a difficult decision given the humiliation. I really wasn't attending the university to be an athlete. I had a more important mission: I was studying marine biology. I was going to farm the seas with Jacques Cousteau and solve the problem of world hunger. Four years later, I found myself in a dead-end job as a tech in a medical school teaching lab with low pay and no potential for advancement. There were days on end that nobody knew or cared whether I was even at work, though I always was. On one of those days, I sat down and created a list of things I wanted to do in my life...dreams.

One truth I've discovered about dreams is that if you have to release one, you have the option of replacing it with an even better one. Heading the list was "Go to Africa." It was followed by "Go to the Galapagos." Which was followed by "Become a writer." And then there was a rather private one involving Olivia Newton-John.

A funny thing happened. Within days, I came across an ad in the University of California newspaper for a charter flight to Nairobi, Kenya--the exact spot in Africa I wanted to visit. And within five months, I found myself boarding a small charter jet in Paris, bound for Jomo Kenyatta International Airport.

You have probably read about the power of writing such lists. I can only tell you that I made this one before having read any of a number of books advocating writing down your dreams and aspirations. Every item on that list has come true with the exception of never having even met Ms. Newton-John, let alone...well, never mind.

There has always been that dream list with additions--and occasionally deletions--over the years. This book is about one fairly recent addition and it chronicles a life, and

IV

even some historical events, that have taken place during that pursuit. This is probably the dumbest dream of all to have ever made the inventory. It did not leap onto the list--it unfolded, like one of those booklets of postcards you see at the souvenir stands along the rim of Grand Canyon or at Disneyland. After the first half acre was planted as a home vineyard, a second followed, and then another...

This story is a spiritual adventure, often mystical, at times profound, and very often just plain weird. All events are true.

I have, in the process, discovered that releasing a dream makes room for even better ones. And that even abandoned dreams have their value. I probably held on to that one about baseball longer than I should have. This was confirmed by the amount of air I moved around the rest of that batting session.

It helps now to know that the pitcher went on to play major league ball. He eventually was elected to the Baseball Hall of Fame and is now included in most lists of the top twenty pitchers of all time. His name was (and still is, actually) Tom Seaver. What he did to me that day he also did to some of the best hitters in baseball. Maybe I should have stayed around to see what the second pitcher had? Naw, I also had no arm. I understand, too, that Mr. Seaver now also has a winery. Oh good...

From Eden, April 5, 2008

Chapter 1

A Labor of Love

A squeak...a chirp...a pitiful bark that sends a bolt of electricity into the heavy, great green-gray fog of deep sleep. It's two a.m....I think...the watch face is a blur. I had started planting that week and had fallen into a near coma, exhausted. There is a saying about country living, that you know you have become adjusted to it when you hear a strange noise at night and just roll over and go back to sleep, hoping that whatever it is has gone away by morning.

But this noise came from the garage under my upstairs bedroom and had special significance. I was out of bed as if the heating pad had shorted on the mattress springs, staggered as consciousness caught up with the rest of me...blinking awake, eyelids of lead, seemingly cemented shut...stubbing my toe on the step up to the hallway.

The evening before, I had ushered Virginia into the garage after her water broke. No, not my wife, a two-year-old yellow Labrador retriever...pedigree: Virginia Woof. I name all of my dogs after famous authors. I had mated her with my chocolate male, Jean Paws Sartre, and it appeared that the long-awaited day was here...or rather, night...or, more accurately, early morning, as if accuracy was remotely possible given my state of mind at that time of...day?

I stumbled down the stairs, nearly stepping on the blissfully sleeping father in the mud room, and switched on the light in the garage. Virginia was lying on the sheet I had placed in the whelping box constructed for the event. Her tail wagged in greeting, wagged some more as I approached. She was so good-natured, tail always going.

At first I didn't see it: the first born. But every once in awhile, there was a weak little squeak. It was hidden in the folds of the sheet. My god it was small. Not bigger than a mouse. It was black. The genetics of Labrador coloration is complex and a yellow and a chocolate breeding can produce yellow, black, or brown puppies. I had hoped for chocolates or yellows.

I had prepared as much as I could. I was surprised--frustrated--that someone had not offered some sort of class like Lamaze for dogs. I had served in the army as a surgical tech and had participated in a number of births and C-sections, in addition to the Lamaze-assisted births of my own two children, but was still annoyed that there wasn't more birthing education available for dogs. With human birth, you have a whole team of professionals and a hospital to help. Here, forty miles from the nearest vet, it was just me and a tail-wagging, valiant yellow Lab.

Let nature take its course had been the vet's recommendation, though he did allow that there would be some benefit to tying off the cords...if I wanted to bother. So there I was at two o'clock in the morning with this black little mouse, a spool of cotton thread, and hands whose fingers were almost as big as the mouse...uh, puppy. This puppy had no previous experience in birth and was not holding very still so that fencepost-size fingers could tie a loop around a toothpick-sized umbilicus.

I looked over at Ginnie with some exasperation. Could she have picked a worse time? She wagged her tail, sensing my exasperation. My exasperation gave her a sense of achievement. She was delighted...wagged her tail some more, and produced puppy number two. I hadn't finished with number one yet. Nor had I when number three came along. All blacks.

I had pestered the veterinarian to give me a count of expected puppies. He had performed an ultrasound, as I didn't want to expose Ginnie or the puppies to X-ray radiation. His estimate was for seven. After the third, Ginnie took a break, allowing me to catch up with my knot tying--or not tying. I found that it worked best if I first made a loop and then "lassoed" the cord. There seemed to be some organization forming. We were doing this! And, as I had been informed that delivering a litter can go on over a period of a dozen or more hours, and all had been attended to, I went back to bed.

But not for long. Noise in the garage. Back down the stairs in a cycle that would be repeated several times over the next eight hours. Number four was a chocolate. A female, I thought...but at less than an hour old, it wasn't easy to tell. I was new at this. I wasn't even that sure of their color. Virginia was a terrific mother and proceeded to wash them all.

The sun came up sometime during this routine. There were ten puppies (three more than the vet had predicted), five black and five chocolates, no yellows. Virginia got her breakfast (which was more than I got), then returned to her pups.

There was a logistics problem in that there were only eight spigots. Even on day one, the larger puppies began to demonstrate their dominance. The two biggest were full-time feeders; they even sought out and won the best spigot. I had to remove them so that the two who were pushed aside could feed. There was a great sense of responsibility for the welfare of all, and an army medic's dedication.

Later in the day, Virginia took a break from the hungry brood and was walking with me in the front of the house, when she began to deliver one more. But this one wasn't breathing. I cleared the mucus from the pup's airway (first step in CPR, my medic training). Then I thumped it with my finger, hoping to stimulate the heart and breathing. No response. Damn. I tried it again, a little harder. Nothing.

Stillborn pups are a common occurrence in the kennel world, but I was a new initiate to this realm and took it very personally. Pretty sure of defeat, I called the vet to ask if there was anything more I could do and also to get directives about the afterbirth that was still retained. I had to cut the cord but was instructed not to pull on it too hard, because it could cause a hemorrhage. What the hell was too hard? I am always breaking bolts when working on my truck because I torque too hard with a wrench. I had no idea what too hard was with a retained placenta. It wasn't helped by Ginnie's incessant tail wagging. That dog was something else.

The vet invited us to come in, even though it was after-hours at the office. So I made a travel box for the pups, as I didn't want to leave them, made mom comfortable, and we drove into town with the setting sun. Ginnie wagged her tail in appreciation and reassurance.

The next few hours were surreal, as the wonderful dedicated staff took over. Virginia still had two more to deliver, they determined. They were going to try to induce labor; otherwise a C-section was in order. For probably the first and only time in my life, I was grateful for my military training. I understood fully what was going on medically and felt very tired, and ten times more than that I felt guilty. I had wanted to have a litter of pups and had put Virginia in jeopardy as a result.

In addition to the vet--the wife of a husband-and-wife practice--four techs stayed on...all female. They had all worked a full day and were also tired. I was sleep deprived and twice as fatigued as any of them and consequently a little heady. The scene was almost like a living dreamscape. Wearing medical greens, the staff infused the air with a sweet scent of maternal care, working quietly without speaking, as if what they were doing was as natural as breathing...bottle feeding the pups, attending Virginia. I was feeling very much the foreigner in this, very much the gender inferior...it had the air of a witches' covenant--albeit very benevolent witches. In my fatigue it was fascinating, intoxicating.

The ten pups were nourished, but Virginia still retained the other two. It was nearly ten p.m.; almost twenty-four hours had passed since pup number one. As they prepared the OR and Virginia, I was asked to wait in the reception room. Despite my training, they preferred that I not participate in the surgery. I was grateful and crashed on a vinyl-upholstered bench, drifting off to sleep though wracked with guilt, thinking about what I had done to my dog by putting her in this situation.

I was reminded of one emergency C-section in the army when I was on call. It was a breech birth and the mother went into cardiac arrest. The word *team* took on an organic, social definition. We were appendages, extensions of the surgeon's skill. The training and experience of all was accentuated logarithmically with compassion. I was just a two-year draftee, grateful that I hadn't been made a machine gunner. I had graduated from training at the top of my class and, in the process of making the most out of the two-year stint, had decided to just do the best job I could. I was circulating, the one responsible for supplying those in sterile gowns--the surgeon and two nurses--as well as the anesthetist with whatever they needed.

When the mother went into cardiac arrest, what was needed was two more people circulating, more sponges, special instruments, and the sterile crash cart with the electric paddles. The baby had to be quickly sacrificed and removed, and the afterbirth that had fallen on the floor had to be picked up, which I did without thinking with an ungloved hand on my way for more supplies. The mother lived and eventually recovered. Afterward, we cleaned the operating room in near silence, with everyone exhausted, feeling a mixed sense of relief and failure and compassion. I drifted in and out of sleep on the veterinary reception room couch with that memory, praying.

Although the remaining puppies were stillborn, Virginia returned to service in a matter of hours. I was amazed at her recovery. I lifted her from the back of the truck gently, not wanting to stress the sutures. If the puppies' eyes had been open, they would have been happy to see her. They greeted her with open mouths, however. She went right to work, feeding her brood, while I stood by to swap out the biggest for the runts.

Now, in my spare time, I could go back to my planting. It was just a home vineyard, about three-quarters of an acre, just over six hundred plants. When the basement of my house was being built, I had planted about fifty fruit trees. I then got the idea of putting in a small vineyard, to make home wine. Although the house, a five-year do-it-yourself project, was still in need of finish work, I was at least living in it. The grapes could be growing as I finished the house, I reasoned. That was before I "lost it."

Ten years later, the house is still undergoing "finish work." And there would be a dozen times when I myself would come close to being "finished."

Chapter 2

Vino 101

I cook with wine,
sometimes I even add it to the food.
--W. C. Fields

The summer after my college graduation, I went to Europe and discovered wine. I understand that most history books have neglected to report this fact. They are too busy trying to convince Native Americans that Columbus discovered America. While turnabout may be fair play, in the interest of avoiding perjury I concede that others before me had made the discovery. I was not the original discoverer of wine. There were indeed vintages that preceded my landing. The European summer marked the entry of it into my life. And on a personal level, it was a significant breakthrough.

Traveling student class meant youth hostels and *pensions* (private homes that rented rooms to travelers) and small hotels that occasionally featured more occupants per square inch than Calcutta. I spent three months there for a sum less than some wine vintages now sell for in the half-bottle.

The restaurants were also of the student or working-class standard. Included in the fixed-price menus, at both lunch and dinner, was usually a half carafe of wine. Of course, I didn't want it to go to waste, so I usually drank it. The wines were not memorable, but they did contribute to the enjoyment of the meal and to the congeniality in general. To one not accustomed to drinking wine, the conviviality often continued well on into the afternoon, and added immeasurably to touring.

Each country offered a new culinary dimension and wines that were equally diverse: in France pâtés and cheeses, an impromptu picnic with a street-vender quiche and Beaujolais; in Spain tapas (small diverse hors d'oeuvres such as olives, shrimp, or maybe a slice of ham) with a glass of *tinto*; in Italy the pastas and *minestras*, which were, to my taste, regal fare. Maybe it was just that cheap wine there was better than cheap wine in the other countries, but even a few slices of salami with Chianti and a loaf of bakery-fresh bread was a delight to consume while sitting in the shadow of the Coliseum.

If I made any one discovery or conclusion then, it was that wine is meant to be consumed with food--even if it is just some cured olives. Actually, I have found olives to be an excellent accompaniment when tasting wine. And restaurants that serve a small dish of them or a tapenade win my heart even before I've seen the menu.

The initiation was not disciplined and occasionally disastrous...a bad bowl of bouillabaisse in Marseille or squid in its own ink at a tapas bar. And occasionally the education was very embarrassing, such as ordering a steak in a little seaside village south of Genoa. The price quoted was a unit price--per 100 grams--not the total price. They weigh a steak and charge you a multiple of the price accordingly.

That education blew the food budget for a week and far exceeded the usual contents of a thin wallet. But the understanding proprietress trusted me to return the next day, when the banks were open to exchange some traveler's checks for lira. In fact, as I recall, she even allowed me to have dessert on credit. It would have been the easiest thing in the world to have scammed her. I could have hopped the next train out of town, but she trusted me to return. Which I did. I love Italy; it is the happiest culture on earth. My affinity for that culture (including the wine) is life long...and maybe beyond. If there is reincarnation, I would like to come back next as an Italian.

Two years after my first trip to Europe, I was fighting the Vietnam War as a draftee in San Pedro, California. I was recently married, and except for having been drafted and earning $75 a month, life was relatively normal...relative to stomping around in rice paddies with an M-16. My reputation must have preceded me, however; for during my entire tour, we were not once overrun.

We had a little apartment with an ocean view, if you leaned way out over the balcony. The balcony also supported a little hibachi, a one-square-foot charcoal barbeque. Wine did not enjoy nearly the popularity in America that it does now. There were small ethnic markets that catered to the Greeks, Italians, and Portuguese who made their living from the sea. And they often offered inexpensive wines from their respective countries. Some bad, some not so bad...the operative word there was "inexpensive." One day, while shopping for cassette tapes in the PX, I noticed a couple of cases of something called Cabernet Sauvignon from a fairly new California winery under the Mondavi Label.

The contents of those bottles marked the beginning of a revolution in the wine industry no less significant than the storming of the Bastille or the Boston Tea Party and should be so recorded in our history books. I was not accustomed to identifying wine by the grape. Médoc, Burgundy, and Chianti were familiar names to me, but What the H was a cabernet and was it always sauvignoned? Most wine from California had been sold in jugs previously or in square, ornate bottles whose contents were sweeter than pancake syrup. The Mondavis did for wine what Franklin, Washington, and Jefferson did for the original thirteen colonies. And considering what has evolved in Washington, D.C., during the last century, the contribution was far more constructive.

I purchased that first bottle for just under five dollars (PX prices), which in those days was at the upper end of our wine budget. The bottle had a cork, which distinguished it from most California wines at the time. But being worldly customers of ethnic groceries, we had a corkscrew and extracted the stopper in one piece. The "Star Spangled Banner," the "Fratelli d'Italia," and the "Marseillaise" blew out of that bottle. That wine was terrific. A few cubes of sirloin, some mushrooms, tomatoes and bell peppers on a skewer, a tossed salad, and maybe a rice pilaf, and the tsars and all of the kings George and Louis would have been justifiably envious. In the culinary realm, never has so much ever been owed by so many to so few.

Wine information for the general public has come a long way since then. Some cookbooks offered suggestions. There were a couple of "bibles." But I often found that I didn't agree with them, that I sometimes violently disagreed. Today, if you Google "wines to accompany steak" you get thirty-four instant hits. We've come a long way, baby.

There was of course the maxim: white wine with fish and fowl, red with meats and heavy tomato sauces. But I am one who goes out of his way to keep his maxims to a minimum. Mine is: *There are no hard and fast rules to wine. Wine is discovering what you like, not being told what to like.* Sure, if you have a big red, say a Cabernet Sauvignon, with a delicate filet of sole, you just wouldn't taste the sole, it would be overwhelmed. And if you have a light Chardonnay with pasta putanesca, you might as well be drinking distilled water. But I also like a nice deep red Sangiovese (the grape in Chianti) with my scampi, and I believe that Pinot Noir was invented for duck.

More recently, before I moved to my ranch, I took a viticulture and enology class through the UCLA extension program. I had just purchased 160 acres of bare ground that had been occasionally barley farmed. And I had no idea what I was going to do with it. I thought when I enrolled in the class that I was going to learn something about making wine. I did--for the first half hour. We were taught a little about the economics. "If you want to make a small fortune in the wine business...start out with a large one," the instructor professed. He did not coin the saying, but that was the first time I heard it. And it did make an impression...albeit not a permanent enough one, it would seem.

It turned out to be a wine-tasting class. And what I got out of that class was more valuable than any wine-making instruction. I learned about pairing food and wine and about how one variety can be so different from vintage to vintage and from winemaker to winemaker. The class had to be held off-campus because of the serving and consumption of alcohol. We were invited to bring "snacks" to go along with the tastings. Mine were usually rather Spartan, often just some crackers, maybe some cheese, as I often attended a class en route to and from my recently purchased property. I think one time I took pretzels. The class was composed of mainly upwardly mobiles who had already mobilized more than I still have, or at least they gave that impression. They came with little wicker baskets and jars and tins and little Saran-wrapped plates from delis that were works of art.

Before each class, there were a number of glasses set at each student's desk, and then the instructor, a wine buyer for a chain of specialty, high-end grocery stores, would pour about an eighth of a glass from several different winemakers. The big ones, the Chardonnays and Cabernet Sauvignons and Pinot Noirs, took two classes. We were introduced to comparisons of French vs. American oak, and those with and without malolactic fermentation (a bacterial secondary fermentation, responsible for the buttery quality of wines, most notable in Chardonnays) and the dozens of other variables, such as the areas the grapes were grown in and under what conditions.

Here is a terrific exercise and one that you *can* try at home. By sampling six different offerings of the same variety from as many winemakers, you will find one or two that stand out and also make the food taste better. In turn, the food will enhance the wine. It becomes a little like a tennis volley: wine enhances the food, the food enhancing the wine.

The instructor knew these wines and so we were given a wide range of flavors as well as prices. Afterward, a vote was taken with each student registering their preferences. It was *never* unanimous. There was rarely a majority winner. If there were six wines served, maybe two or three would garner the most votes spread evenly. Invariably, I voted for the cheapest and the most expensive. Sometimes the vote was entirely even. Rarely did one go without any votes. Some might say that this is due to ignorance--that if certain vote casters knew anything about wine, they would not have selected the one they did. And it is my firm belief that those who would say that should be pitched headfirst into the nearest spit bucket. If you say you like chocolate ice cream over vanilla, you don't have some snoot looking down his nose at you as if you had just created a bad odor. If that happens to you with wine, just tell him to go trim his nasal hairs and bring you what you want.

My second cardinal rule of wine appreciation: *Wine is learning what you like, not being taught what to like.* My first cardinal rule? *There are no cardinal rules in wine.* As I would discover, this pertains to its making as well as its consumption.

Just to retrench a bit here before I am sentenced to a lifetime of bits of floating cork by a conspiracy of offended sommeliers, most wine-serving professions today (and this includes merchants) are eager to assist and really are there to support your preferences. There is more of a team spirit of having fun with wine than there was in those days when I was still in the army and my new bride and I were hosting her elderly godmother in a restaurant known for their wine list. A white that hadn't been cold stabilized was uncorked before I noticed the crystals in the bottle.

The sommelier threw a tantrum when I requested a different wine, and even when I said I would pay for the first (to be doggie bagged) he created a scene. The wine is not damaged if it sports these crystals. I had some vague knowledge of this then, but had just preferred not to impose the wine on our guest. We eventually got another wine, but we ended up leaving before finishing the meal anyway. Not because of the wine, but because of a rather brutal earthquake that ensued, raining plaster on us all, and the subsequent severe nosebleed that the godmother suffered. The wine with the crystals was consumed the next day and the godmother recovered, but the restaurant, never again to be revisited, was left with no tip and with table linen probably thereafter rendered unusable.

That class of sommelier has all but gone the way of the *Tyrannosaurus rex*, and more recent experiences have produced some great pairings where I have been unfamiliar with the wine list but was able to communicate my preferences. And there have been times when I have ordered a wine that the server was unfamiliar with and have either requested an additional glass for them to sample or left a bit in the bottle for their subsequent after-hours taste.

The instructor at that UCLA class was not a wine snob; he believed that you should have fun with wine. So in addition to setting my determination not to start a winery (not having even a small fortune), the class reinforced that aspect of wine: to have fun with it, to seek out those tennis matches. I guess those who I refer to as the sip-and-spit school, who gasp when you have an opinion that is not theirs, are having fun, too...in their own way. I gave them a gasp opportunity and the rest of the class, particularly the instructor, a good laugh when, as the last meeting was coming to a close, I thanked him for the enjoyable class. "I really learned a lot," I said. "Before taking the class, I hadn't even known that you were supposed to take the bottle out of the paper sack."

Chapter 3

Planning a Home Vineyard

Terroir is Not a Small Dog or a Reaction to the Nursery Bill

As the puppies and their mother were getting along famously, I was able to get back to planting. Virginia was a terrific mother. In spite of having a six-inch, fresh, and probably tender suture, she nursed her brood attentively. They were now almost twice as big as they had been at birth and looked more canine than rodent.

The bare-root vines that I was planting were purchased from Sonoma Grapevines, the foremost supplier to the wine industry. I had met with their representative the previous winter, during a three-day seminar on viticulture in Sacramento. His name was Dan Roblado, and in spite of the fact that I was planting only three-quarters of an acre and there were vineyard managers planting thousands, I was accorded the same attention and courtesy as the big guys. I would not always find this to be true when it came to contractors and suppliers. Dan even visited my site prior to planting, and when about five plants did not survive the first year, he made good on the company guarantee and replaced them.

The Sacramento event was sponsored by UC Davis, the mecca of viticultural academia, just fourteen miles down the road from the seminar site. This was my scholarly introduction to the cultivation of grapes. Almost taken for granted at the conference was the necessity of planting grafted vines, where the grape producing variety is grafted onto a Phylloxera-resistant rootstock. Phylloxera is an aphidlike insect that is transferred in the soil and roots of infected grapevines. The sap-sucking insect feeds on the roots, girdling them and gradually cutting off the flow of nutrients and water to the vine. Virtually pesticide resistant, the bug originated in the United States and was responsible for nearly wiping out the vineyards of Europe, as the Europeans had reimported vines from the United States in the 1860s.

Ironically, the roots of native American grapes are resistant to the pest, but their grapes do not produce drinkable juice. Grafting European vines onto American roots solved the problem. UC Davis has added another refinement by producing certified disease-free vinifera (the grape- producing top half) as well as rootstock. As most of the world's vineyards are now planted with certified, grafted vines, it was nearly a foregone conclusion that my three-quarter acre would be, too. At about five dollars a vine, the approximately six hundred vines represented no small investment.

For the selection of varieties, I looked to the local wineries of northern San Luis Obispo County and southern Monterey County. Some of the best Zinfandel in the world comes out of Paso Robles, about thirty miles south of my ranch. Zin was a natural choice. Because the climate here reminds me so much of Tuscany, and Chianti is my personal favorite, I also looked to those wineries that produce Sangiovese (the main ingredient in Chianti). Climate is only one aspect of *terroir*, which is basically the vine's total environment (including the cultivar type itself). There is an initial desire among some new growers to duplicate Napa, California…or Burgundy, France. Each encompasses dozens of terroirs that in some cases are defined in vine rows. I knew I didn't live in either place and that trying to emulate them was futile.

I looked to Paso Robles and Tuscany for guidance. It is hot here in the summer. It is not rare to have a few days above a hundred and ten degrees Fahrenheit. We get almost nine months of what many places call summer. Being one small coastal range from the coast, the nights are cool and sometimes foggy. And the soil is poor. But poor soil can inspire the vine to produce some excellent fruit. There is an old Italian saying, "The poorer the soil, the richer the vine will make you."

Cabernet was not put into the shopping cart; neither was Chardonnay as I was looking for a unique niche. I opted for Sauvignon Blanc as my main white (as there were some fine local examples) with a few experimental vines of then–little known Pinot Gris, also called Pinot Grigio (it's not exactly suited for here, but I was curious). I also chose to plant the not highly regarded Tuscan white, Trebbiano Toscano. I hold it in higher regard than most do and find it a great complement to grilled fish and poultry. Also, it is a legal ingredient in Chianti. Finally, I planted a test block of about forty vines of the exotic-sounding Malvasia Bianca, one of the grapes that are made into the ambrosial Italian dessert wine Vin Santo. This grape is also used in Chianti.

Once the varieties were chosen, the work of deciding what to get was only half done. In poring over the lists from a grape nursery you will discover an array of "clones" for each variety. There are dozens of almost every variety to choose from. It's a veritable candy store.

To help decide which ones to plant, I turned to the local wineries--and got some surprising responses. Most of these vineyards were older vines, own-rooted and Phylloxera-free, though not resistant. There was also a common opinion that a little disease, such as leaf curl, was actually desirable...with the stress of the vine contributing to the complexity of the wine. "Beautiful vineyards don't always produce beautiful wine," was the maxim delivered by John Munch, then the winemaker at Adelaida Cellars winery and now owner of Le Cuvier, both in Paso Robles. John took an entire afternoon to escort me around his vineyards, expressing his philosophy.

As he made one of the best Sangioveses, I listened attentively. He was a major influence and I am indebted to his generosity.

What you will discover if you delve into wines and wine making is that there is never unanimity. For every opinion, there seems to be an equally qualified opposite opinion, just as in the consumption. Recall that class at UCLA where there was rarely agreement about the best tasting. That same disagreement seems to exist about how to *make* the best tasting. A majority of new vineyards plant certified vines. The nurseries that supply the big plantings offer predominately certified, grafted clones whose source is UC Davis. Most lending institutions will not lend money to uncertified, ungrafted vines. And most big wineries will not hazard a large investment of their own for something with a higher risk of failure. Disease-free offers lower risk, and those vineyards are indeed putting out some fine wines.

However, yielding to the wisdom of John Munch, I did order about fifty vines that were grafted but whose vinifera was not certified. It was viable, I was assured, but mildly diseased and consequently less vigorous than certified varieties. I also made a decision that probably betrayed, possibly portended, that I was already looking beyond a home winery. I selected a variety of rootstocks as an experiment to see what might grow best here and to help determine any future plantings. Any future plantings? The warning about making a small fortune in the wine business was already being swept into the oblivion of sound thinking. Whatever else this was, it was fun.

Chapter 4

A Field of Dreams...
With Two Hundred Place Settings

Your first job is to prepare the soil. The best tool for this is your neighbor's garden tiller. If your neighbor does not own a garden tiller, suggest that he buy one.

--Dave Barry

Growing a single grapevine is not a difficult assignment. You dig a hole, insert the vine, preferably root down (sometimes difficult to tell with bare-root), fill in the hole, and add water as needed. If you are going to plant two grapevines, you will need to give them a couple of feet of breathing room. And if you are going to plant six hundred grapevines, and you do not even have a small fortune, you are going to need to have a strong back and a feeble mind.

When a large vineyard is started, the land is usually ripped with several large blades the size of your leg, drawn by huge tractors that resemble mechanical Jurassic Park escapees. The objective is to break up the hardpan layer to give the roots a fighting chance. I found out about hardpan when I was planting my fruit orchard. While my basement was being constructed, I planted fifty fruit trees. I carefully marked out five evenly spaced rows and drove short stakes into each prospective tree location as markers. The first couple of shovelfuls of dirt pealed off of the top. At about one foot the going got a little tougher. The shovel penetrated another six inches. And at two feet I thought I had discovered the foundation of a temple from an ancient civilization. The shovel could barely scratch the stuff; the handle bowed. I poured a bucket of water, let it soak in, and tried again. Another six inches. At that rate, it would have taken about a year to plant those fifty trees, so a backhoe was brought in and two-foot-wide, three-foot-deep trenches were dug in a half day. The trees eventually did very well and have provided a bountiful harvest every year since, which the birds and squirrels occasionally share with me.

The backhoe would have been overkill with the smaller grapevines, so a posthole driller with an eight-inch-diameter auger was brought in. The idea was to get through the hardpan to give the roots a chance to grow down and spread out. At about a foot and a half we hit the hardpan foundation of the Anasazis. A foot more and it was rocks and bits of cement like earth, which continued for another foot, and then another. It must have been an Anasazi fallout shelter.

The auger had a depth limit of six feet, but we gave up before that. It had taken almost a half hour to go as far as we did for one vine. Times six hundred, at fifty dollars an hour, the no-small-fortune was going to become the national debt--certainly a personal one. And since I did not have a congressman's salary, I made the decision to dig two-foot holes for the plants and three-foot holes for the posts. The roots were just going to have to fight their own way beyond that. If that old Italian saying, "The poorer the land, the richer the vine will make you," was true, I was sitting on a gold mine.

To mark the hole locations, I used plastic picnic spoons, knives, and forks. The vines were spaced five feet apart on rows eight feet apart, with holes every thirty feet for posts. It looked pretty funny seeing the white plastic field of tableware (anticipating future pairings?). I decided to emulate John Munch's vineyards with pressure-treated wooden double posts, cross-braced, at the ends of the rows, and the same wooden posts every thirty feet along the length to help support the trellising.

If you think there are a variety of opinions about wine tasting and about variety and clone selections, then there will have to be a new word coined for the diversity of opinions about grapevine trellising. The third cardinal rule of viticulture is: *For every opinion there is an equally qualified exact opposite opinion.* One of the speakers at that first conference in Sacramento was considered to be the godfather of grapevine trellising. There was an audible hush in the auditorium when he took the stage--the Dalai Lama of posts and wire.

The purpose of a trellis is to support the grapevine. Once supported, you want to get light to the fruit. I have to admit that I was lost as the speaker and his monks had these cat's cradles going out over the vineyard that would make great snares for prehistoric monsters. For my purposes, I was going to use two wires running from end post to end post, one high and one low that would double as support for the drip irrigation line.

Oh, yeah, another source of varied opinions: how to get water to the vines. This can range from none (dry farming) to sprinklers to the most common, which is some form of drip irritation...uh, irrigation. This also has a rainbow of opinions. Basically, it is a hose with an emitter inserted at each vine that drips water to a thirsty plant at a regular, slow rate, usually less than a gallon per hour. As my home vineyard was relatively flat, I went with a one-gallon-per-hour, free-flowing emitter, one to the plant. And thus I developed yet another cardinal rule of grape growing that also applies to wine appreciation: *I reserve the right to change my mind at any time.* And I would...frequently.

Chapter 5

Planting

I'm a great believer in luck and I find the harder I work, the more I have of it.
--Thomas Jefferson

It looked for all the world like the surface of the moon or a field with a big gopher problem (really big gophers) or a fairway after I had played golf there--on a good day. A dozen rows of fifty holes pockmarked a small sector of previously open field.

The arrival of that first box from Sonoma Grapevines was momentous. It was heavy cardboard with hand holes in each end of the three-foot box. The vines were wrapped with plastic to retain moisture. But when you open it, don't expect a thing of beauty. Grapevines nurseries are not florists. Inside the plastic-wrapped liner, tangled and black from overwintering, were 250 dormant bare-root vines. They were bundled and tied with string; a tag identified the clone.

Even with the plant holes and postholes predug, there was a lot of shovel work. The gravel and shale had partially refilled the auger holes and had to be removed before inserting the plant, then refilled...then watered. The drip system hadn't been put in yet, nor the posts. After about six were planted, they were soaked with two gallons of water from a garden hose. To protect the plants, half-gallon waxed cardboard milk cartons open at both ends were used. These were purchased in bulk and came flat and unfolded, the tops and bottoms adding to the total height, which was about a foot and a half. These offer protection from direct sun and keep marauding rodents from eating the young plants.

Life couldn't have been any better. The puppies, at four weeks, were a lot of work, but never had work been so much fun. When the door from the house opened, they charged to the nearside of the pen in greeting. I was attacked when I went into the pen surrounding the whelping box. They absorbed attention, sought it out by nipping at my ankles--or toes if I was barefoot, which I wasn't as soon as they started getting teeth--or pulling at my belt loops if I knelt. And then woe be it if I had any kind of tool, like a screwdriver, protruding from my pockets. They could pick pockets as well as any Artful Dodger. And you wouldn't even know the article was missing until a tug-of-war broke out over it…sometimes a full riot. I made the mistake of leaving the broom inside the pen one day, and returned several hours later to find a handle and straw lining the kennel.

I had to clean the kennel three times a day, but when a doggy door was installed that led to a small outside "run," almost to the pup they would use it to go outside for the deposition of puppy treasures. After their meals, and after cleaning the kennel and run, I would sit inside and sacrifice my arms and legs to attack. And they would climb up the ski slope of twelve-pack abs and try for my eyewear or earlobes. At night we would have story time. With bellies full, they would gather around or "on" as I regaled them with the tales of King Kong Kitty. It wasn't long before they were all asleep. I have been told that my stories have that effect.

Virginia was such a terrific mom, I took great care not to exclude her. She almost went into ecstasy when I would pet her. She was so proud. And the pups learned to get out of the way of the wrecking crane tail as it wagged. And the dad? He was pretty oblivious to the goings on in the garage. Likely as not, you would find him in the house fast asleep flat on his back, spread eagled, snoring. Dogs enhance a life the way that wine enhances food.

The grapes got planted in spite of the ten puppies. I hadn't put in the drip system, yet (we are talking about the grapevines here). If this story is ever made into a movie like *Sideways*, it would be aptly entitled *Backwards*. There is a great advantage when growing grapes in having your ground prepared and water system in place before you start planting. I was watering six hundred grapevines with a hose, one plant at a time. I had to get the drip system in. The nearest water connection big enough to handle six hundred gallons an hour was three hundred feet away. Add on to that another sixty feet of manifold to feed each row. That's a lot of digging.

When I built my house, I did all the trenching for electricity and water, probably over a mile of it, with a rented trencher. I felt quite capable of doing this myself, but I had been referred to a local guy, an assistant fire chief at nearby Fort Hunter Liggett. He seemed an affable sort, and when he said he could do the job for less than if I rented a trencher, his affability soared. I probably would have hired him if the price had been higher. How could I not hire a guy to trench my vineyard irrigation lines with a name like Doug Waters?

One of my favorite topics is Synchronicity: serendipitous coincidences that at times can border on the profound. My take on them isn't that they are some significant life-altering sign. A road sign, maybe, like the mile markers telling you that you are going in the right direction, just a little happy reassurance. When the DeeJay came on the radio as I was varnishing some doors and said, "It's a good day to paint a door," I just had to laugh. It was a good day for it and the doors came out great. Doug Waters became a lifelong friend. He also got the pick of the litter, choosing the one female chocolate.

Now with the vines being watered with the twist of a valve, the milk cartons seemed to work pretty well as the vines began to leaf...so far, so good. The cottontails seemed attuned to the symbiosis as the watering was also bringing up grasses. And in the morning they would venture out of the brush line to within a few feet as I worked, to nibble on the previous day's weed growth without disturbing the contents of the milk cartons. Even the quail found the disturbed, wet earth to their liking and joined the bunnies in the vineyard. Add a fawn and Walt Disney could have made this into a movie. I didn't know it then, but I was being lulled into a sense of false security. The Trojan horse was inside the then unerected gates. I would look back on this scene with cynical amusement. Tranquility can be an elusive state in the country. And, as the vines began to climb over the tops of the cartons, I was about to discover that if this was a movie, it wouldn't be made by Walt Disney. And probably could have been written by Stephen King.

Chapter 6

Paradise Lost

There is nothing more miserable in the world than to arrive in paradise and look like your passport photo.
--Erma Bombeck

Just when you think that you have things going all your way, life has a way of humbling...humiliating...infuriating. Going out one bright morning to start the irrigation, something was missing. You don't know what it is at first and then realize it is about twelve vines. A quick investigation--the contents of the milk cartons are intact, the leaves full and bright green, but where the branches emerge from the tops, everything is cut off. The cut is ragged--chewed. Rabbits. During the night, they had discovered that the succulent young new grapevine growth was more to their liking than the new grass that grew around the vines. There is a feeling of betrayal. They had been provided with rich greens that wouldn't have been available to them otherwise. They must have had an orgy. The treaty was over.

Rabbit tacos aren't one of the items you will find included among the recipes I like to pair with wine. It's only because I believe that they go better with beer. But I can attest to the excellence of the dish, and for the next couple of days it became a staple. Diced and sautéed in olive oil and garlic, it is remarkably like chicken. Inserted into a freshly fried corn tortilla with cheese, lettuce, and tomato it makes for sweet retribution as a one-inch mesh wire fence is begun around the vineyard.

Meanwhile, in the kennel, Virginia was having her own problems. One of her breasts had become infected. So we had to make another "quick" trip into the vets. They are forty miles away, so "quick" means something like an hour each way and an hour and a half there. Half a day shot: fence construction halted. The infection wasn't serious. She got some antibiotics and instructions to keep the pups off the infected breast. Oh, good, now only seven spigots for ten puppies.

When we got back, it was just in time to see a bunny scamper out of the vineyard. But what was worse, we were greeted by a pack of roving puppies. They had broken out of their kennel and were delighting in the wide-open spaces of the front yard. I had to park the truck down the drive for fear of running them over as the pack ran hither and yon much like a K-division soccer game. This was not a good thing, in spite of what they might have thought. They were small enough to be delightful snacks for some of the predatory birds, and there were coyotes and bobcats that were a concern for even the adult dogs, not to mention the rattlesnakes. Their father Sartre, aka Farfo, had been bitten several months prior.

It had happened at night, and because the rattler usually beds down at night, I thought he had just been stung by a bee or wasp; probably from his drinking water, as the wound was on the inside of his mouth. The next day, a Sunday (dogs in the country never get sick or injured when the vet is open), his face and neck were terribly swollen and for the first time in his life he seemed very contrite and humble. That required a drive of seventy miles to the emergency veterinary hospital, where he was put on IV solutions and kept overnight. He recovered completely. But he had been fully grown.

Virginia also had her own serpent encounter when she was still a puppy, soon after I had brought her home. The night before, I'd had a dream, a surrealistic dream about a pipe-cleaner dog, a little, fuzzy white dog made out of pipe cleaners. By some miracle that can only happen in dreams, the little toy was struggling to be a real-live dog and stand up. But it was using whatever life force it had just to gain its feet. The scene was just outside on the back step of my house, by the doggy door. I felt a great sadness; it was using all of its life force just to stand. I admonished the poor little thing that it was alright. It didn't have to stand up. I urged it to lie down.

The next day, I was reminded of the dream in a fit of urgency. This time, I was trying to get my real-life white Lab to lie down. She kept trying to get up and I ordered her down to "lie down, god-damn-it, lie down."

Outside of the doggy door, where seconds before she had run right past, a three-foot diamondback rattler was coiled, tail buds buzzing. A rattlesnake does not rattle, it buzzes. For those who have not heard the sound, it is very similar to the sound that a large grasshopper makes, or a dragonfly or a hummingbird. But the sound of the rattler is more sustained, louder and has a different, unmistakable timbre--of anger and danger. Perhaps if a grasshopper or hummingbird were angry and twenty times bigger, the sounds would be identical.

I first had to get my dog to stay put. I wasn't sure if she had been struck. Blissfully ignorant of the danger, she had just run right by the serpent.

The only way in or out of the dog yard was through the back door. I had to convince Ginnie to stay put, then get my twenty-two, which was loaded with birdshot rounds, and then get back to the snake before Virginia did.

Somehow these dogs always seem to know when to listen. Like the little dog in my dreams, she would not stay down. But she at least remained in place...sitting. It was a compromise I was willing to accept. I wanted to get that snake before it took cover. Seconds later, I slowly opened the back door, while repeating the order for Virginia to "*Stay*!" I didn't want her anywhere near the line of fire as I eased my rifle through the slightly opened door. The universe's rattlesnake census was diminished by one. Country living--never a dull moment.

The funny thing was that as I came back in, having tossed the snake parts out of the yard, I noticed, lying on the back step, a used pipe cleaner. Although I had previously been a pipe smoker, this was during a time that I had sworn off tobacco and hadn't smoked for several months. How that pipe cleaner got there, at that time, I will never know. Nor did I know then how prophetic the dream and story would become. Suffice to say, the story is illustrative of the hazards of country living of which the new pups were blissfully ignorant.

The puppies mobbed me as I stepped out of the truck. They tried to climb my legs and bit my sandaled feet: "Ummm...toes." An exercise was begun that would be repeated more and more frequently over the next few weeks, a count: five black, five chocolate. They were unscathed, all here. And there. And then over there...

Chapter 7

The Best Laid Plans

Everybody is ignorant, only on different subjects.

--Will Smith

Perhaps life's most reliable lesson is that plans never seem to work out the way you envision. Apparently I am not alone in this. You have heard John Lennon's "Life is what happens when you're busy making other plans" or Woody Allen's "If you want to make God laugh, tell him your plans." I have a penchant for making people laugh--at, as well as with-- whether in the supermarket checkout line or in a classroom. I even made Clint Eastwood laugh when I met him. I would like to think that God (or my preference, The Infinite Unknown) is in the audience.

The puppies contributed one more divine comedy hour of their own. There was a saying among parents that I commiserated with when raising a family that God invented teenagers so that you don't feel so bad when they leave home. The same might be said for ten-week-old puppies. They were old enough to leave home and between vineyard and kennel activities, the owner had also aged in doggie-years. Still, letting go wasn't easy.

It helped that the first pup went to Doug Waters, who selected the only chocolate female. I knew she would be well cared for. And when Doug's adult son selected one of the blacks, I was equally reassured. Two down and eight to go (seven if I kept one). And before I could even get two to be photographed for the local Photo-ad, one of Doug's firemen claimed a pair for his family and another went to the owner of the feed store that we had been subsidizing. There was a brief hope that maybe there was a potential for a business here raising Labradors. According to the mental business plan, there was going to be a positive cash flow for the first time on my ranch even after the vet expenses for Virginia and all of the initial shots and other puppy preparations. But was that thunder I heard or laughter coming from the grandstand of angels?

The two puppies I took to the photo session became ill. At first I just wrote it off as upset tummies, but when they became lethargic, I grew more concerned. And when, on the second day, they showed no interest in food, we packed up immediately for another trip to town--to the vet.

The diagnosis wasn't the most terrific. They had Parvo, a highly contagious viral infection that attacks the digestive system. At one time it was almost always fatal but great strides in combating it had been made. The vet held the two for several days under his care with instructions and medication for the remaining dogs, including the parents.

The adults never developed any symptoms and the three pups at home developed only very mild symptoms. Happily all were to recover fully as the two hospital patients were returned. And if I had any misgivings about letting go, I was given a reprieve: they were quarantined for several more weeks at the Spa Del Corvo. The two chocolates were dubbed Stan and Oliver, the three blacks were Larry, Moe and Curley. And if life had been a comedy before, it achieved a new standard of hilarity as the puppies gained their health at the expense of mine.

Led by the one I had originally dubbed Houdini, now Moe, the pups were not to be contained. And as they gained weight and size, I had misgivings about being able to find the more mature rascals homes. I had visions of being the proud, permanent owner of seven dogs. But this was not to be, thankfully, as two pairs were purchased at a slight discount in price. And as the car containing the last two disappeared down the driveway, there was an agonizing sense of loss, not only to see them go, but also financially—those vet bills had removed any remote chance of positive cash flow. Gee, I guess, the wine business isn't the only way to do that.

I took solace in the companionship of my more manageable three-count kennel: Sartre, Virginia, and...oh, my god...it was Moe/Houdini, the bane of my existence. There was a moment of realization as we stood at opposite ends of the side yard, in a Gary-Cooper face off at high noon. The day was still and we each stood our ground in silence. Then he bucked playfully and ambled toward me with the most winning happy face that any dog has ever presented. He would prove himself one of the most affectionate, intelligent—and consequently, at times independent—and also most loyal dogs I've ever known. He would get one last formal name, for his AKC registration, in keeping with a tradition of using names of literary figures and also acknowledging his jet black coat: Vic *Tar* Hugo.

I have chronicled some of my plans gone awry and actually this book may be about one big one. But I have also seen that putting out wishes often brings unexpectedly rapid results. My desires to become a baseball player or a marine biologist never bore fruit. And now it seemed that starting a kennel would join those. However, sometimes even more far-fetched ideas--following the heart--often have seemed celestially accelerated. How I got to Africa for example, or even how I landed here on this parcel of property. An addition to the vineyard was about to come in a like manner.

The experience of living here is replete with wishes come true, often seemingly out of thin air. I recount some of these in my earlier book, *WALDO*. As a problem would arise, a solution would shortly follow. When I was building my house, for example, I had not given much consideration to the finish flooring. And when the building inspector wanted to see the kitchen floor finished before final inspection, I had no idea what I was going to put down. The next week, on the news radio from San Francisco, some two hundred miles away, I heard an interview with a group at Fort Ord, some eighty miles away--where I had taken basic training three decades before. They were disassembling the barracks and selling the building materials. That turned out to be the source of the flooring in the main part of my house: beautifully aged and distressed seventy-year-old Douglas fir.

The solution to an empty triangular plot of ground inside the rabbit-fenced vineyard was about to be filled in a similar manner through some unlikely assistance. It would come from my electrical supplier. Guido Dusi and his partner Gary Kircher owned Paso Robles Electric. I first met Guido when the framing was complete on my house and I was ready to start running the wiring. I encountered the superficial gruffness of a professional electrician faced with a know-nothing dolt, owner-builder amateur. Part of his façade was a defense mechanism, protecting a heart of solid gold that was vulnerable to being taken advantage of. I saw through that right away, and as I presented my building plans, I also perceived a subtle softening. I had drawn them myself. I had built the house 90 percent by myself. I had done this without electricity, living for five years in a little trailer, depending on a generator to run my saws and drills. As I did with most phases of construction, I submitted my plans to several suppliers for bids. Within a week, I returned to pick up my first load of wire, electric boxes, control panels, switches, and outlets.

Throughout the electrical installation, how-to questions would arise. And always Guido addressed them with professionalism and years of experience. Sometimes my questions drove him to the brink of exasperation. I still have the diagrams he drew of the installation of three-way and four-way switches: the correct way to have a particular light fixture operated from more than one switch in different parts of the house. These were clear and precise, so that even an amateur dolt could follow them. Almost a work of art, I recently had them framed as a memento.

Several months after my electrics were in and running, I happened upon Guido as I was jogging along Ramada Drive, just south of the town of Paso Robles, on my way to the outdoor equipment auction that is held there. I arrived a couple of hours after several dozens of other prospective buyers had, and parked up Ramada about a mile and a half. I was late for the scheduled tractor auctions and was in a rush...anxious that I would miss it. I started to trot. As I came to the magnificent old-vine vineyard, Guido was driving down the driveway. Surprised to see him there, I stuck out my thumb in the style of Clark Gable (or so I envisioned), hoping for a ride the last quarter mile. He threw open the passenger door. I was a little out of breath, and short chunks of conversation were exchanged before he dropped me off at the entry to the auction: Yes, he knew the owner of the vineyard; it was his brother, Benito.

I did not buy a tractor that day. But within a week I was driving up that driveway with an introduction to Benito Dusi from his brother, passing vines that could have been subjects for a Van Gogh painting. The Zinfandel vines had been planted by the father of the brothers, seventy-five years earlier; their trunks were as big around as trees, gnarled, twisted, free-standing vines--head trained and spur pruned. Having lost their leaves as midwinter approached, they resembled bonsai trees, three feet tall.

Benito was walking up his drive to the house. Under his arm he was carrying a newspaper, the *Wall Street Journal*. As I pulled up alongside, I was surprised when he extended it for me to read. It seemed a little incongruous to be reading this publication while standing in the center of forty acres of old-vine Zinfandel. But the anomaly was dispelled as he pointed to the article on the inside back page. It was a retraction of an earlier piece, an apology, and ran nearly a third of the sheet. Apparently the previously run story had blasted the quality of Zinfandel wine. The writer, a noted wine journalist, had become better informed (wine is learning what you like, you know) and now showered praise on the variety. Leading his list of picks was one made from the old-vine Dusi Vineyards of Paso Robles. Benito presented this with the pride akin to that of a kennel owner after hearing how treasured his puppies had become in their new households.

The citation in print served to confirm two hunches: the acceptance of Zinfandel as a world-class wine and that these vines, grown in this region, were capable of producing that wine.

There used to be a little wine bar in Paso Robles called Busi's (with a *B*) Chianti Room. It has since been sold and transformed into an Irish pub. Before, when it was still the Chianti Room, there hung a large, old sepia photograph of three men standing in a vineyard holding glasses of dark wine. The three were Mr. Busi, the elder; Mr. Dusi, father of Benito and Guido; and Amadeo Peter Giannini, founder of the Bank of America and hero of the recovery from the great San Francisco earthquake and fire of 1906. Standing there, reading the article Benito handed me in the *Wall Street Journal*, I was surrounded by American wine history.

Benito, with the generosity that I have learned to be second nature to his whole family, gave me permission to go out and collect cuttings. "Leave three buds," he instructed, meaning not to cut too close to the main trunk, permitting next year's growth.

If my cargo that afternoon had been ingots from Fort Knox, it could not have been more precious. Since I didn't have a greenhouse, I cleared out part of the basement of my home. Using leftover building materials, I set up benches to support several flats of four-inch pots filled with Supersoil. In each was stuck a three-bud cutting. I installed two banks of grow lights suspended from the basement ceiling and plugged them into a timer. The cold water pipes were exposed and it was a simple matter to install a spigot for a garden hose. For a minimal investment, I was in the business of propagating grapevines. The words of the instructor of that wine-tasting class never far suppressed, I rationalized that I was just filling a bare spot in my vineyard. I reflected on the absurdity of it, laughed at the production facility that would have gladdened the heart of a marijuana grower. That endeavor probably would have been more economically justifiable. Instead of a few hundred dollars' worth of grapes, I could have had a five-figure crop of pot. But as the buds began to break and the dry little twigs were transformed into plants, fiscal reasons seemed to be an inconvenience to be ignored.

Chapter 8

Spirit: at the Root and Rout of Spiritual

In the long run the sword will always be conquered by the spirit.
--Napoleon Bonaparte

(Yeah, but his father probably didn't wear a belt...and it is probably a good thing that mine didn't wield a sword. kfj)

When I was still commuting from Los Angeles to the newly purchased ranch in Monterey County, there were basically two routes you could take. The fastest route was all inland and less scenic but cut about a half hour off the drive. Where Interstate 5 winds over the mountains north of the San Fernando Valley, the long, steep path is known as "the Grapevine." Rock and roll fans will recognize the name from "Hot Rod Lincoln." At the bottom of "the Grapevine" there is actually a huge vineyard. Frequently, the oldies station would play the tune "I Heard It through the Grapevine" as I would descend into Kern County.

Now some might say that it was a sign. Perhaps it was. It happened with some regularity. I didn't take it as such, however. I didn't drop everything I was doing and start planting grapes. My three quarters of an acre didn't happen until five years after I had been living on my ranch. I just took it as one of those little coincidental road signs, but more prophetic than some.

The second route I would take was the coastal route, the Ventura Freeway, as many as five traffic lanes in each direction, cutting through the suburbs of greater L.A., then breaking out into the open coast just south of Ventura as Highway 101 in a long graceful curve from almost due west to due north. It is a great gasp of fresh ocean air and is a little startling as you make the transition from city to coast. Where the vistas had been of a continuous string of suburban communities, shopping centers with either a Burger King or Taco Bell, you are now suddenly presented with the unending brilliant blue sun-glare vastness of the Pacific.

As a small boy, I had lived slightly further north right on the water at the base of Rincon Point. It was a wonderful association with the ocean. In those days only a couple of houses were there. It is now a community with streets and a gated entry, and the waters have become renowned for the surfing in what was once my front yard. Two of the bungalows, a matching pair, had been built by Warner Oland, one of the actors who played Charlie Chan in the movies in the 1930s. When we lived there, he had since passed on. But even then, the highway was only two lanes wide. Today, the freeway passes right over where our house stood, and its construction was the reason for our moving.

As I was about to plant those cuttings from the Dusi vineyard I had an opportunity to stay in one of those bungalows built by Charlie Chan. It turns out that they had been converted to a bed and breakfast. Walking that beach, forgotten memories flooded back: the fog, the texture of the sand, the tar on the beach from the offshore oil, and how the bottoms of my feet were scoured with lighter fluid to remove it before entering the house. Four-year-old feet are tar magnets.

A footprint in the sand, not human like in *Robinson Crusoe*, but a dog's--a large dog's--takes you back decades: Gretta, a huge Doberman that had belonged to some Filipino farmers. She couldn't bark, something with her vocal chords wasn't right, and she was horribly infested with fleas. She loomed over me like a horse. She was my first dog (part time).

The saying "You can't go home again" was particularly apt, as my home was under what is now the southbound lane of U.S. 101. Sitting on the huge rocks that serve to keep the ocean from washing away the highway, on top of the site where our house was, looking back at the bungalows that once stood alone, I remembered this view from the sunroom where my mother read to me when it was raining.

On returning to the ranch from this boyhood sojourn, the memory floodgates still open, I got to thinking (one of the great untold advantages of physical labor is the chance to think) about how complicated the influences of life foundations can be, and how they are manifested later on-- whether it is in plant cuttings or puppies or humans. Some of the cuttings grew with a flourish of health. All seemed to get the same light, water, and nutrients, but some just grew faster, and then went on to be the biggest plants and later the most prolific producers of fruit.

But I found out that they don't necessarily produce the best wine. A smaller plant produces less fruit, and the fruit it produces has a smaller, more intense berry and contributes a far more interesting quality to the wine. A couple of the puppies are bigger and more assertive, but one of the mid-sized ones (Hugo) develops a greater curiosity than the others and probes at the confines of the kennel. He becomes the leader--and troublemaker--as the pack follows him on a prison break. I can look back on those years at Rincon and marvel at the influences: the love of the sea, leading to the study of marine biology; a love of dogs; the affection for the written word that probably came from those early introductions to *Heidi* and *The Overall Boys*, but out of it also came a great sense of self-reliance and independence. I loved to explore, and was also a handful.

One early expedition from that time comes to mind. We had gone to my grandparents' house in the suburbs of Los Angeles for a traditional Easter celebration. My grandfather was Russian and took great pride in his spicy potato pancakes, served amid platters of ham and painted hardboiled eggs. My parents were active in the church and participated wholeheartedly in the religious celebration. But two sessions of Sunday school and then the first full Easter service in the main church were about all that a four-year-old could take. Thoughts of a brightly colored Easter basket full of candy that included a huge chocolate bunny just overwhelmed the prospects of attending a second full service. I'd had all of the redemption and salvation that I could possibly handle and determined to return to my grandmother's on my own. Here was the sprouting seed of wanderlust and independence that would bloom in my later life as a travel writer, and also the roots of the antipathy for those who attempt to restrict freedom of travel.

The distance between that Easter basket and church was about two miles: eight blocks south and twelve blocks east. We had driven it dozens of times. In retrospect, it was not a trip appropriate for a tyke, across uncontrolled, busy intersections. Before the invention of the crosswalk, it was dangerous. One of my grandfather's adult brothers was later struck by a car while crossing one of these streets and killed. But that day, I was luckier.

The streets were lettered and numbered. I remember vividly watching the numbers decline on the streets I crossed: 17th, 16th....When I got to 9th Street I did not cross. This was the street my grandfather lived on. Although he lived on the opposite side of the street, I didn't cross. You had a better view of the other side of the street from there. I turned left, looking hopefully for familiar signs of the block I was normally restricted to. It was over a mile away and when the two towering pines in the front yard came into view, it was a great relief. But mounting the front steps was an ambivalent triumph...somehow this wasn't going to be all the victory I had planned but rather my first appearance on God's Comedy Central.

My grandfather, thinking I had been dropped off by a parishioner, let me in without ceremony. Two hours and several chocolate eggs and marshmallow bunnies later, the phone rang. It was an old-fashioned phone where the earpiece hung from a cradle on a pedestal topped by the microphone--like the ones you see Humphrey Bogart use in the movies. There was a gasp, and silence, and then an ominous change in grandpa's demeanor. A storm had been building that all too soon would unleash its full fury in the form of my father and his belt.

It seems that the entire congregation had been on a manhunt, or rather a boy hunt. I had *disappeared*, at least from their point of view. It never occurred to them that I had just gone home. Four-year olds couldn't--wouldn't--do that. The police had been summoned. There was the fear that I had been kidnapped or was, at best, just plain lost. All of which puzzled me. I always knew where I was and wasn't lost at all. But I would soon wish that I had been. At age four, I was the recipient of one of those corrective measures that society in the form of a father's belt imposes. As a result I do pay attention to admonitions that might result in corrective measures such as warnings about large fortunes turning into small ones.

I had no intentions of becoming a commercial winery. I also had no idea how successful that first propagation of the Dusi cuttings was going to be. About 90 percent of those first rootings took. I needed plants for about a quarter of an acre and there was nearly twice that amount growing in the basement. Uh-oh.

Chapter 9

Old Dogs, Children and Watermelon Wine

I don't like country music, but I don't mean to denigrate those who do. And for the people who like country music, denigrate means 'put down'.

--Bob Newhart

In the spring, my uniform is Gore-Tex. A favorite jacket, purchased for hunting, fends off the water; and it is down filled, cozy even when pounding stakes during a hailstorm. Working in such weather can be a frolic, as long as the stones are kept under a couple of carats. Light boots, also of Gore-Tex, are preferred to heavier ones; accumulated mud makes them heavy enough. Flannel shirts and jeans, changed several times a day when it is raining lightly, round out the wardrobe. When it is raining hard, it is usually best to just wait it out, otherwise road crew or sailing foul-weather gear is in order.

When it was cool to be a hippie and wear flannel shirts, I was a yuppie, in button-down shirts and Weejuns. Now that it is cool to be a yuppie, I find flannel shirts, with a turtleneck underneath, the mainstay of the wardrobe...talk about being out of sync. And stocking caps, under the Gore-Tex hood of that jacket, are the ultimate in comfort, as you slog, gleefully in contempt of the weather. And it doesn't hurt to have a radio turned up to the country western station. When I am writing, I like classical, sometimes oldies rock and roll. But outside in the vineyard, C-W just seems appropriate. Music enhances work, the way that wine enhances food.

For the basement-reared vines, improvements were made in planting efficiency. If you lay out the irrigation lines <u>before</u> planting and give the drip lines a few hours, at a gallon an hour, you can dig fairly easily until you hit the hardpan. Instead of drilling holes at a couple of dollars a hole, you can just use a shovel to excavate a six or eight-inch repository for the rooted plant. You don't have to go down to the hardpan, and the work is fairly easy.

As difficult as it may be for the reader to believe, there are two opinions about dealing with the hardpan. There is the main school, which advocates bringing in the dinosaur rippers to tear up the earth to great depths to destroy the hardpan. And there are those who scoff that the hardpan will re-form in a couple of years and you will lose most of the benefit of ripping. "Let the plants fend for themselves" is their motto. There are different kinds of hardpan, some almost nonexistent, whereas mine is harder than the I-5 pavement. The drilling of holes for the nursery vines was an attempt at a compromise--short of ripping, but giving the plants a shot at getting through it. But the ground under the hardpan where I was planting was not much different than the hardpan itself...rocks and gravel. Not having the funds to pay for the dinosaurs or for more hole drilling, I thought I would see what the vines could do on their own, becoming a de facto member of the second school, but with reservations.

Reserving the right to change your opinions and methods is as common to viticulture and enology as it is to the consumption of the end product. Ask enough questions and eventually you find a solution that works best for you. Even the measure of what is working best is a matter of perspective. Some measure their vineyard in tons per acre. Others determine results by what happens when you uncork that bottle and there is a whiff of grape and alcohol, which becomes more erotic as the color manifests in the first splash in the glass. If it is a white wine, it pours clean and clear and promises to quench more than thirst, with hints of exotic fruit or vanilla. If it is a red, it slides down the sides of the glass like glycerin, even climbing up the other side, growing darker with each dram, almost black, the glass properly funneling the aroma, traveling all the way to the back of the palate before the mouth has even become involved with the liquid. There is a promise of intoxication (in the overjoyed, seductive sense as differentiated from inebriation), intoxicating like Lauren Bacall's eyes, peering through a shock of hair in that movie where she teaches Humphrey Bogart to whistle, not drunkenness.

If you have had the wine before, you might know what is coming next; if this is the first time, there is anticipation; and if you are lucky the texture is sensuous. The liquid slides to the taste buds (which only disclose salt, bitter, sweet, and sour) but joins forces with the olfactory senses, producing a gasp of gratitude: appreciation like for a Mozart composition or a Van Gogh painting.

I didn't care how many cases, bottles, tons I got. I just wanted to make something that enhanced a grilled steak; and something for salmon; and something for garlic, tomatoes, olives, and mushrooms with pasta. And in turn to be enhanced by the fare after the first sip, and well into the meal when you leave just enough room for dessert and you still want to applaud. Finally, a light, sweet glass of a dessert wine, like the triangle that chimes at the end of a symphony. That's sorta what I was after. This was a home vineyard, right? Economics weren't a factor.

But first things first. I hadn't even produced a grape, let alone made wine.

As I was getting ready to plant the vines from the basement, the ones from the first year needed to be trained. Grape growing is a lot like firefighting. You have to decide which fire needs to be put out first. I had ordered some extruded metal stakes from a local manufacturer. The first cardinal rule of dealing with suppliers when you are planting less than a few acres is that you cannot depend on good service. I could provide a list of farm and vineyard suppliers and would soon be able to add wine-making suppliers that really don't give a hoot what or when you get the stuff you need. Instead, I will offer up names of those that are the exception and get return business. It's my money, and until I get more than promises not kept, it will stay that way.

As the year-old vines got thrashed in the winds, I was waiting for the stakes ordered from a local company with the big display ads in the trade and wine magazines. After being promised they would be here from week to week for several weeks, I gave up on that big-name supplier. I had to resort to what I then thought were inferior rods from Jim's Supply Company in Bakersfield. Not as local, but certainly no small concern. When their representative, Mac Anderson (now retired), drove out the next day with a couple of bundles of rods, I was so grateful, I am mentioning it now some ten years later with undiminished gratitude. The rods worked fine and I have used them ever since (they are also less expensive). For training young vines, you don't need more. The delicate young vines being whipped around in the wind were given the urgent added support that they needed...and not too soon.

A metal rod or light rebar pounded into the ground also serves to support the plastic grow tubes that Mac also introduced me to, and which quickly and permanently replaced the milk cartons. The translucent grow tube also serves as a mini greenhouse, retaining the heat and still allowing in light. It also offered about a foot and a half more height protection from rabbits as a few rows of those extra Dusi vines were planted outside of the fence. Planting outside of the fence? The floodgates had been opened.

Chapter 10

Where the spirit does not work with the hand, there is no art.
--Leonardo da Vinci

People love chopping wood. In this activity one immediately sees results.
--Albert Einstein

As I surveyed the extended rows from the basement-rooted Zinfandel--"the Annex"--I had a wicked sense of joy. I'd gone outside the boundaries of the fenced-in "home vineyard." Five more rows, staked and grow-tubed, almost militarily neat, like stacks of gold coins...value, assets. The value a vineyard adds to the land has been quoted at twenty thousand dollars an acre or more. There is now more than one acre planted. The basement-rooted plants alone represented a little over a quarter of an acre. That translates to five thousand dollars of increased value, give or take. All for a couple of hundred dollars worth of stakes and cones and a lot of time (OK, so maybe ten thousand dollars worth of time—but the real compensation is in the satisfaction in the results of the work: physical, hard, honest work.).

Adjacent to the last five rows, there is a fairly flat area, about an acre in all, before the hill drops off into pure gravel and wild brush. You toy with the idea that maybe a few more vines could be added alongside them. Those last rows just look a little lonely there, a little out of balance. Like a board sticking out of a roofline. But instead of cutting it off, you add a couple more and make a sundeck. And if you have some extra grapes (the law permits one hundred gallons of wine per person, per year as a home winery) well then maybe you could sell them.

This illogic began one of the happiest, most encouraging experiences of generosity since moving to the ranch. I began polling wineries that made Sangiovese and Zinfandel well. Some didn't return my phone calls. But some did, and one of the most fortuitous was contact with a winemaker at Robert Mondavi. A lot of water had gone under the bridge since that first bottle of Cabernet Sauvignon purchased at the PX. The name Robert Mondavi had become one of the foremost in the industry. Now it's a legend.

Although I have never met the namesake, I have to believe that the people I talked to at his winery are a reflection of the quality of the man as much as is the quality of his wine. I was reminded of my stepfather, probably the best man that I have ever known, who built a very successful business of high-precision valves and filters around his designs as an engineer. He often said that he didn't build a business, his employees did. They were enthusiastic, dedicated, and talented and, in turn, ultimately very well compensated. My stepfather's secretary, who in the early days had to go without a paycheck because there weren't any funds to pay her, became the CFO when the little company became a publicly traded one. She retired a multimillionaire...and she did it before there was a feminist movement.

The telephone receptionist at Robert Mondavi was courteous, and instead of taking my number with an empty promise of having my call returned, as several much smaller concerns had done, she connected me to Jim Moore, then an assistant winemaker. He was intimately involved with the Mondavi wineries in Italy and was preparing to visit them in the next couple of days. Wineries in Italy? Here I am counting vines by the handful, and have an audience with a corporate executive about to be jetted across the Atlantic on what most mortals would count as a dream trip, who counted acres of vines by the portfolioful. He was affable and enthusiastic about the possibilities of creating wine made from California-grown grapes that would compete with the quality of the best of the Italian grown. The term Cal-Ital has come to encompass this effort for wines from Chianti (Sangiovese) to Vin Santo (the dessert wine made usually from Trebbiano or Malvasia Bianca). "Yes, I have a Sangiovese that I like pretty well," Jim told me. "I can send you a bundle of twenty-five at a dollar apiece." There was some urgency in sending him the money because he was scheduled to leave for Italy, and so I sent off a check that day.

A couple of days later, I got a call from Jim Moore. He had received the check and wondered why it was made out for thirty-five dollars. "For the shipping and handling," I explained. We hadn't discussed that element and I was hoping the extra ten dollars would cover it to avoid any delay in sending out the vines. "Not enough?" I asked, hoping that there wasn't going to be a delay in getting the cuttings.

"No, that was included in the twenty-five dollars," he said.

"Oh, well, if you have more cuttings, I could use them...I just appreciate your help," I replied.

"We'll work out something," he assured me.

When the box of cuttings arrived, it was like Christmas as a kid. My standard pocket contents when working in the vineyard include a utility knife. This was produced deftly like a gunslinger drawing in a showdown at high noon, and with only slightly less enthusiasm. I precisely sliced the wrapping tape along the edges of the flaps of the cardboard box in a moment no less momentous than if the contents were the Holy Grail or the Arc of the Covenant. Instead of these, I found a neatly tied bunch of "sticks" but also...a bottle of wine...the top Sangiovese produced by Robert Mondavi, whose retail price was more than the thirty-five dollars I had sent. "We'll work out something," I mused.

There were also more sticks than I had been promised. And they were nearly two feet long, with enough buds to make three or four plants per cutting. Ultimately, I would plant five rows of twenty-five vines per row from these cuttings. In the meantime there was a spaghetti dinner enhanced by a bottle of wine whose memory will forever be cherished (the empty bottle now a table ornament), for the generosity and also as a standard. I hoped that the wine I would make someday from those vines would hold to that quality. An event that seemed to be so remote in the future.

Chapter 11

The Root of the Matter

The love of economy is the root of all virtue.
--George Bernard Shaw

Up to this point, all of the vines planted from cuttings were own rooted. I was just rounding out the home vineyard, a majority of which--now about half--had been nursery-grown, grafted vines. The planting had all been miles away from any other wine grapes and the hope, if not the logic, was that the ranch was sufficiently insulated from Phylloxera, which is transferred through the soil. That did mean that any equipment, from shears and shovels to tractors and discs, had to be carefully screened and any soil removed. Doug Waters always power washed his tractor or trencher before even coming over. Even shears from off-site were given a chlorine rinse before use.

As the Mondavi cuttings started to sprout in the basement, I began to research rootstocks and also enrolled in two viticulture classes at UC Davis, the academic center of all things agricultural in California. By now, it was becoming quite clear that growing wine grapes had become a passion-- at the very least, a passionate hobby. I just liked doing it: taking cuttings, potting them, caring for the young plants, planning the vine rows, and planting. I was guarded against the *W* (winery) word. But maybe I could sell grapes and grape vines. If I was going to do that on any larger scale than my now one-plus acres, I thought I would have to be grafting onto rootstocks. But which ones?

The original grafted vines had been selected also for the variety of rootstocks. I wanted to see if any rootstock had a higher success rate or offered better support for the soil and climate of my ranch. Judging from the now two-year-old vines, it appeared that all were successful. The vines were flourishing and were being trained to cordon wires. One question did remain unanswered and that had to do with grape production and grape quality. A few valiant vines had put out a scraggly cluster here and there, but you can't even begin to hope for any kind of crop until the third year.

The instructors at Davis weren't able to offer definitive answers. Bear in mind that UC Davis specializes in producing disease-free vinifera and rootstock. There is a vested interest in proselytizing for the virtues of their research results. You might be forgiven for being suspicious of a teacher who states that "healthy, disease-free vines produce healthy and disease-free grapes, superior in quantity as well as quality," when winemakers you respect tell you otherwise. This instructor went on to say that quality wine did not even depend on the clone of any given variety and that "a good winemaker can make any one of these into a superior wine." The implication was that healthy vines produce great wines in the right hands; and if they don't, it's the winemaker's fault.

As some of the best wines in the world are now made from certified vines, there is support for such statements. But echoing in my memory were the words of more than one winemaker, "Pretty vines don't necessarily make pretty wines." As did the second-to-the-last page of the *Wall Street Journal* that cited the wine made from the Dusi Vineyards, whose seventy-five-year-old, own-rooted vines are not disease free, even suffer from some Phylloxera. I do recall hearing somewhere that no matter what opinion you encounter about wine making and grape growing, you will find an equally qualified opposite opinion.

While at Davis, I spent my lunch breaks in the university bookstore. Bookstores in general have always been venerated, as have libraries. When I was in high school, I lived a couple of miles from the Huntington Library, one of the world's richest troves of ancient documents that includes such august publications as the Gutenberg Bible and Shakespeare's first folio. On rainy days I used to ride my bicycle over there, where I would have the place to myself to browse the displays, to wander in the estate's gardens, and to gaze in amazement at the floor-to-ceiling shelves of leather-bound books in the main house.

The viticulture and enology section of the university bookstore was like a double shot of fudge to a chocolate junkie. One of the pearls that I picked up there was *Vines Grapes and Wines* by Jancis Robinson. As this passage is being written, I picked up the book for reference, trying to arrive at a fitting description of that text. Enthusiastic sincerity and industry of research to back it up is apt. There is no doubt about her enthusiasm for the subject of wine, but what she offers is not just a salon or saloon assessment of the beverage. She also knows the vines and the varieties--even to the clone level--and the regions and climates. Remember the instructor at UC Davis who said that clones are not significant? Quoting from the book's section on Sangiovese: "Clones can be even more important than climate."

I have had that book for a decade now, and I still dive into it like a kid on Christmas Eve with a toy catalogue. That she is also an excellent writer doesn't help, and if I don't return the book to the shelf, I will spend the rest of the afternoon in it instead of finishing this chapter.

When I was trying to decide which rootstocks to plant, I didn't find much on the subject in the book. So I did what any journalist would do, I went to the source. I called her on the telephone. I don't even remember how I got the number--attribute it to journalist's creativity. The connection wasn't very good. "Is this Janice Robinson?" I asked. "It's Jancis, yes," came the patient reply (Jancis not Janice). I glanced at her book, realized that I had already gotten off to a not-good start. But I was exuberant with the success of having made the telephone connection. I knew that the question I was about to pose was tantamount to asking Mozart what keyboard ivory source he preferred or asking Shakespeare about his favorite ink. But she was affable and genuinely interested in the question. What was her opinion on the relationship of wine quality to the rootstock?

The conversation lasted several minutes and ranged off the subject of grapes to also include writing. Perhaps that I was a writer, too, helped. She said that she knew more about the relationship of soil types to appropriate rootstocks. She also pointed out that some noncertified vinifera did not take well to grafting at all and were best planted on their own roots. The Dusi and Mondavi cuttings came to mind. Maybe I had actually done something right. I was juiced that she had been so generous with her time. One of my life discoveries is that the bigger some people are, the bigger they are.

Jancis has since gone on to star in a PBS series on wine and has produced several more definitive volumes on the subject. She signed off by wishing me good luck, and I suspect she knew how much I was going to need it.

Chapter 12

The Wine of Art Making

Making good wine is a skill; making fine wine is an art.

--Robert Mondavi

I had tried to make wine once, long before I ever even had the ranch. I had ordered a can of wine-grape concentrate and a plastic fermenting bin through the mail. And, six months later, I took the bin around in back of the garage and dumped it out on the ground. It isn't that you can't make wine that way. But I didn't. There are a lot of things that can go wrong when you make wine, but the basics are not that complicated. You take sweet grape juice and add yeast, and the yeast turns the sugar in the juice into alcohol.

Simple enough, huh? But there are extenuating conditions that can influence this very simple process. One is the quality of the juice. And then there are wild yeasts and bacteria that can turn the juice from the finest grapes into something akin to turpentine. Temperature and air are two other variables. Once the fermentation has finished, air becomes the winemaker's worst enemy. If you have ever opened a bottle of wine and left it uncorked for a few days, you know what air does to wine.

Winemakers have a lot of enemies. Bacterial contamination is another, so you want to have sanitary working conditions. Potassium metabisulfite is the solution of choice for sanitizing. Chlorine bleach also works, but you

60

have to rinse it out well before exposing wine to anything sanitized with it. Sniff a bottle of bleach and you will know why.

Most commercial winemakers also use potassium metabisulfite as a preservative. I was determined not to. My reason? There used to be a little Italian restaurant near where I lived in Los Angeles that was a favorite of mine. The quality of the food was excellent, the prices reasonable, and they catered to families with kids. They also had a terrific salad bar. In those days it was common to also use a sulfite mist to keep the greens fresh. There is a small portion of the population, however, that is sensitive to sulfites. This great little restaurant had the misfortune of having such a customer who was unaware of their sensitivity and who suffered a severe reaction to the salad and wine combination that ultimately was lethal. It was a great tragedy for all, and the restaurant closed as a result, never to reopen. Restaurants no longer spray their salads, and wines containing more than a micro amount of sulfites now have to show this on the label (actually you have to have wine tested and certified by a lab in order not to have to include "contains sulfites" on the label). Because of this incident and the fact that some commercial winemakers use it in very small amounts, I decided to be one of those to an extreme.

There are some winemakers who consider wine making a science. It is my opinion that it is an art. The scientists-- who make some terrific wines--use a lot of tricks, additives, clarification techniques, and filtering to produce their wine. My approach was to keep it as close to the unadulterated natural product as I could. The first year, I was hell-bent on not using any sulfites at all. This was one stand that I eventually would do no better at than Custer. I sanitized with bleach the first year and rinsed twice with water every vessel and apparatus--even the bins used in picking--that came into contact with the grapes. But no matter how careful I was, I would eventually yield to the pressure to use some sulfites to combat invading microorganisms.

The third year after planting is usually the first year of harvest. You will hear it referred to as "the third leaf" (the third year the plants have leaves). It is wine-grower jargon and does add color to the prose and can add self-esteem to a grape farmer (the guys that pour the wine aren't the only egos in the wine industry). He is called a vineyardist: *Standing out in the vine row, the briar hanging from the corner of his mouth emitting comforting wafts of the smoldering imported Cavendish, insulated from the drizzle in down and Gore-Tex, the vineyardist examines the vines, making a mental note of the quantity of flowers. A sizable number of them for the third leaf, he judges.*

In fact, I had no idea what to expect in production. I had heard that in the third year...uh, leaf...you will get some fruit. Full production from a vine doesn't happen for several years. The Dusi vineyard has vines that are now nearly one hundred years old. Being extremely restrictive in what I applied to the vines--not even using fertilizers--I would learn can add a year or two (or five) to the delay. Still the satisfaction is overwhelming, third behind puppy and child rearing...but not a very distant third.

But seeing those flowers and knowing that they would become grapes and remembering that first wine-making experience with the can of concentrate, I felt like the wafts of Cavendish were disguising the terror. There had been a few rogue bunches the previous year, enough to support the notion that they were grape vines, and there were considerably more now. You just don't want to screw it up.

As a journalist, I had been self-trained to ask a lot of questions. And I did. Especially of those in the business of selling wine-making supplies. Those in the business come to it from diverse backgrounds. In those days, when brewpubs and homemade beers and ales were enjoying a renaissance, a good many of the brew suppliers also sold wine-making supplies...with little more wine experience than what I had. Some had been home winemakers and were expanding their hobbies into a small business.

I had done enough research and asked enough questions to know that I was going to need a crusher/de-stemmer and a press. The first separates the grapes from the stems and slightly breaks the grapes. The latter separates the products from the de-stemmer into juice.

In spite of my best efforts to ask all the right questions and select reliable suppliers, there was one hitch. I was one hundred miles on my way to pick up my imported, stainless steel crusher/de-stemmer, having been informed that the shipment from Italy had arrived. In those days, pre–cell phones, I would check in with my home answering machine. More than halfway to the supplier, I retrieved the message: "Ken, did you want a motor with your de-stemmer?" (The order had included one. A de-stemmer without its motor is about as useful as a brand-new engineless Hummer.) The recording continued, "I thought you might like to know that while the de-stemmers are here, we haven't received the motors yet."

I paused, thinking how I would have liked to have known this the day before when I had called to confirm that the de-stemmer was in...before I had traveled half of the two hundred miles to pick it up. I was glad though to have received the call. As I was halfway there, with my first harvest ripening in the field, I decided to continue on and pick up half of my de-stemmer.

While I stood there in the phone booth, I thumbed through the tattered pages for the number for Grainger. For those who are not familiar with this company, and who have ever even replaced a faucet, you are in for a treat. For those *Tim the Tool Guys* who know the company, now is the time for the elk mating call. A quarter in the slot and seven numbers punched correctly put me in touch with my local store. While they now are online, in those days they had a catalog about the size of a cement block and twice as heavy. I am sure on several occasions just the book alone saved my house from blowing away. I guess the catalog is still available, but the Internet has since saved whole forests by the reduced printing of this tome.

By giving them the specifications for my de-stemmer, the clerk cross-referenced it with several electric motor models. I ended up getting a slightly larger motor than the one not supplied by the wine-making equipment store, and while it wasn't in stock at my local Grainger store, it would be in the next day. I could pick it up on my return from my two-hundred-mile trek to retrieve the other half of my de-stemmer. If ever there was an exemplary model of free enterprise and capitalism, it would have to be that company. Guys standing in foot-deep snow in Montana and in waist-deep water of a flooded bayou in Louisiana, or in the fishing fleets of the Portlands on both sides of this country will nod in agreement about the service that this company provides.

I also picked up a basket press on the trip. The design is classic and harkens back to the Romans. The grapes are dumped into a cylindrical basket and the juice from the grapes is then forced through the openings in the oak slats. A pitcher lip on the rim allows the expelled juice to run into a catch bucket.

Another essential was a refractometer, used to determine the ripening of the grapes. It looks like a short telescope with a stage and a flap on the top. Under this stage is a prism that refracts the light when you place a few drops of grape juice on the stage. Typically a bunch of grapes is pulled from the vine and squeezed into a reclaimed (empty and clean) cottage cheese container (available at any supermarket); the mess is swirled around and a few drops are poured onto the refractometer's stage. The light is refracted according to the sugar content of the grapes and is projected as a colored bar on a scale viewed through the telescope's eyepiece.

The remaining room in my truck was stuffed with white plastic bins and glass carboys for fermentation. I also bought one oak barrel...a five-gallon one.

As I drove back home, I felt like a real wine-making dude: "Get yourself an outfit and you can be a winemaker, too."

Chapter 13

A Watched Vine Slowly Ripens

The two professions are almost the same. Each depends on source material and takes a lot of time to perfect. The big difference is that today's winemakers still worry about quality.

--Filmmaker and winemaker Francis Ford Coppola

There were so few grapes that I began by testing the sugar of just a single grape plucked from random bunches in the vineyard. It may astound the reader that this is not the way to test for ripeness. Typically you select a bunch or two to test (but every bunch was so precious). It is not necessary to check twice a day. I just didn't want those grapes sneaking up on me and ripening without my knowledge. You want the grapes ripe enough to produce wine in the neighborhood of 12 percent alcohol. To achieve this, you have to get a sugar reading of twenty-four degrees Brix (24 grams of sugar per 100 grams of liquid, 24% sugar). For every two degrees, you get 1 percent alcohol. The reading on the refractometer was twelve. And during the month of July it climbed into the teens. In August, the low twenties. And by mid-September, readings were consistently in the mid-twenties.

In the best style of the Keystone Cops, the Three Stooges, and Laurel and Hardy, the first harvest began. The Wal-Mart bins fit perfectly in a little red child's wagon (from Target). It would be christened my John Deere and has become one of the most valuable acquisitions--for planting as well as harvest. The Pinot Gris was the first in. About sixty pounds of them. Then a hundred pounds of Sauvignon Blanc. The whites are pressed as soon as they are harvested. First the grapes are crushed and de-stemmed and the resultant "stuff" is then poured into the basket press and the juice separated from the skins. It became quite clear that it was important to have the catch bucket in place under the press at the outset as a couple of bottles worth of free-run juice ran freely onto the ground. Ollie whacks Stanley in the forehead and jams an empty bucket under the press's lip. From there, it is siphoned or poured into the primary fermenter. In commercial wineries, these are huge stainless steel tanks. On this small home winemaker scale, it is a white food-grade plastic "trash" can.

Red wines, on the other hand, are fermented after crush and then pressed. Red wine derives its color from the skins of the grapes. If you press off the juice of a red wine grape right after crushing, you will get a "white" or rose-colored wine. White Zin, for example, is derived from the same grapes as red Zin. It is just pressed immediately after crushing to prevent the color extraction.

To achieve the color when you want it, the fermented red wine "stuff" from crushing is poured into primary fermentation tanks. From here on out the sugar level is monitored by a hydrometer, which has a potential alcohol scale as well as a Brix scale. Twenty-four degrees Brix equals 12 percent potential alcohol. Then as the yeast starts converting the sugar to actual alcohol, the potential alcohol (and sugar) level drops. As this proceeds, the skins, with all of their wonderful color and tannins, start to float to the top of the tank. You have to push these skins back down into the liquid several times a day so that the wine can extract the color. To do this I acquired a state-of-the-art precision made oak-hewn implement. In the academic world, it is called "an axe handle."

Finally, in about ten days, the yeast has done its job and the potential alcohol is near zero. This means that the wine is 12 percent alcohol. During fermentation, the yeast is producing carbon dioxide. This floats on top of the fermenting grapes, being heavier than air, and protects it from oxidizing. But when fermentation stops, this protective layer dissipates and air becomes the number-one enemy of the winemaker. Fermentation can be quite vigorous. The tank becomes warm to the touch and it sounds like a bowl of Rice Krispies when you first pour milk on it. And there is a wonderful aroma that is a promise of the wine to come.

Once fermented and pressed, the wine has to be stored in airtight vessels, the secondary fermenter. This can be an oak barrel, a sealed stainless tank, or a glass jug (a carboy) like you find at the office water cooler. These have to be filled to the top and a cap called a fermentation lock placed in the neck of the jug. The fermentation locks come in a couple of different varieties and rely on a small volume of liquid that permits any gases produced by the still fermenting wine to bubble off while preventing air from getting in.

Since I wasn't going to sulfite the wine, I had to take great care to avoid contamination. All of the vessels were sanitized. I was using household bleach then, and the results had the fresh, clean smell of laundry, which was scantly better than the dirty socks aroma of spoiled wine. This was the last year I would use bleach. The results were not so harsh on the reds. Just like doing the laundry, the coloreds were separated from the whites.

Staggering down the steps to the basement with the last five-gallon carboy of Sangiovese, you wonder if you want to do this even as a hobby. The forty gallons (sixteen cases) I had produced was slightly less than half of the government-established maximum of one hundred gallons. But whatta lot of work...jeeze. You really aren't sure if what you are feeling is satisfaction or relief. Is it the sense of accomplishment for three years of work coming to culmination, or are you just glad that you won't have to do it again for another year?

But as the cuts from the pruning knives begin to heal, as the crusher and press are put in storage until next year, and as you replenish yourself from the strain of fifteen-hour days, an insidious rejuvenation takes hold.

The writing of *WALDO* had begun, capping a bizarre year of discovery and investigation into the possibility that a manuscript written several years earlier had been royally ripped-off; had become a successful novel, a bestseller; and the movie was about to come out. It may come as a surprise to the reader (it has at times to some editors) but I have always considered writing as my number-one calling. *WALDO* substantiates that in effort, if not in deed. With the wine tucked away, the house a comfortable shelter--if in need of a great deal of finish work--life did seem almost too good to be true. Having work that is rewarding, to do and being accomplished, is perhaps the best meaning of life. And you would think with such a full plate that one would be able to ignore the three acres to the north, a blank patch of land between the house and the water tank, which puts it close to water--pressurized water. You'd think.

Chapter 14

May everything you say or do result in good.

--Tibetan monk valedictory

Plans are only good intentions unless they immediately degenerate into hard work.

--Peter F. Drucker

As the first vintage of some thirty gallons aged in glass carboys, I began inquiries with the viticulture department at UC Davis about becoming a certified nursery. Selling the cuttings from the vines seemed an attractive source of additional income. The material had to be trimmed off annually anyway as part of the plant maintenance. Selling certified cuttings was even more appealing. It isn't a very rigorous process to become a certified nursery. It does require purchasing the cuttings or young plants from UC Davis. In addition, the site (that area between the house and water tank for example) has to be approved to establish that it is free from contamination.

After nearly five years of submitting to inspections during the building of the house, starting another process of being put under someone else's authority on my land was not attractive. The house was built with the intention of far exceeding code standards, and those inspections always went well; the inspectors and I never had any conflicts of interest.

Living in the country does open you up to some suspicion, I guess. Right after the bombing at the Atlanta Olympics, I received a telephone call from a man claiming to represent the company insuring my ranch. He wanted to schedule an inspection. "We just want to make sure you aren't making any bombs," he quipped. I had nothing to hide. I certainly did not make bombs. Not having any prior notice from my insurance company, I thought his "I am coming whether you like it or not" attitude was arrogant. He seemed to imply that I might have the privilege of being insured by the company revoked if I didn't comply. Because I chose to live in a rural location for the quality of life, I resented being even remotely associated with those that did so with less principled intentions. I wasn't intimidated, which appeared to be his intent. "You work for my insurance company?" I asked. I found it hard to believe that someone coming on this abrasively worked for any insurance company. "I work for [name of his company, now forgotten]," he explained. "We have been retained by your insurer to perform the inspection."

I simply told him that I was not making any bombs and was not engaged in any illegal practices, and that if there was a legitimate reason for an inspection, the front doors would be open. But *he* was not going to be the one making that assessment, if indeed it was necessary.

I then called my local agent to inquire if this was a legitimate contact and was informed that such inspections were performed from time to time routinely. I related the events of the previous paragraphs and within a matter of minutes the regional manager agreed to personally make the visit. Several days later, it was accomplished without event, cordially and with mutual respect.

At about this same time, I actually invited an inspection by local and state law enforcement agencies when I discovered some wire fencing "tents" interlaced with branches on a remote section of my ranch. I suspected that someone was cultivating something there that they didn't want discovered from the air. And when I made the discovery, I wanted to make it very public that the cultivator was not me. Had there been any crop (which there was not), and had it been discovered by law enforcement--even if I had not known about it (which I hadn't until then)--I could have been liable for fines, confiscation, and, potentially, incarceration. With one minor exception that inspection (which entailed sliding down a steep hillside in the mud in a spit-and-polished uniform) by a sheriff's deputy (remember, this was at my invitation) went smoothly. The one exception was when I produced a utility knife (used for cutting drip irrigation line) from my bush-shorts pocket to cut some string as we talked. The deputy's hand went to his holster. I stopped still. There was a "gunfight at the OK Corral" moment until I explained the benign intent for the tool/weapon. I apologized for the misunderstanding, realizing that his reaction was part of his self-preservation training. He didn't know me or my purpose. The apology defused the tension...when I set the knife down. Other than that, the inspection went well.

Still, I wasn't looking forward to the visit from the agricultural department. In that experience I would become conscious of a truth that would serve me well for the rest of my life: *Laws and regulations and bureaucratic requirements are not the making of the ones employed to administer and enforce them.*

As the inspector emerged from the cab of his truck that day, he reached back to retrieve a plate of the best homemade brownies, courtesy of his wife, that I have ever had. It was a peace offering from a representative sensitive to the intrusive aspect of the process he was employed to oversee. I took it then and reflect on it now as a magnificent gesture. A rapport was immediately established as we proceeded with the inspection; it was done amiably and with respect but was about to fail miserably in a futile effort on my part to show my appreciation. I was reminded of a maxim learned years before: *The best of intentions don't always produce the intended best results.*

One of my favorite sayings is the valedictory of a Tibetan monk, who ended his lecture with: "May everything you say or do result in good."

I have to smile every time I recall the impossibility of that invitation: how intent and outcome are divinely paired. I digress here to illustrate the learning early in my journalistic career. Then on assignment to cover the Miss America Pageant, I went with some terrible misconceptions, expecting to encounter a bevy of toothsome bimbos. Wrong. And while toothsome--and then some--those women are sharp and directed. And even for Miss Fiftieth Place, it is a great career boost. I would go away impressed.

I was assigned to do an article on one specific contestant who will be here unnamed and referred to as Miss Unnamed State. After my first interview with her, which was chaperoned (as were all meetings), I went on the Atlantic City Boardwalk to shoot a couple of rolls of film. The contestants all had badges with their pictures and state name printed below. I was given one during the interview and wore it as I went out on the Boardwalk, in the spirit of the event. As I stopped to buy some saltwater taffy, I was cornered at the cash register by another customer. She saw that I was wearing Miss Unnamed State's badge, and proceeded to tell me that she comes to the pageant every year and how she thought that Miss Unnamed State was the best representative from that state in years.

Later, at a formal reception for Miss Unnamed State, I mentioned the candy counter encounter. And in my infinite sense of poor timing, calling on my best public speaking voice, whose ability to travel great distances--such as across a soccer field and back in a single bound--I repeated the other taffy buyer's words, the enthusiastic opinion that "she was the best Miss Unnamed State in years." The words echoed throughout the room: "in years...in years."

I was puzzled by the blank look on Miss Unnamed State's face. It wasn't the response I had expected. It was as if I had told an off-color joke to the preacher's wife. I wasn't puzzled long, however, as she proceeded to introduce me to two very attractive ladies standing in a group next to us, well within earshot of the soccer coach's statements. "Ken," she said. "I'd like you to meet Miss Unnamed State from last year," adding as the room went deafeningly silent, "and this is Miss Unnamed State from two years ago."

The same fickle fate of best-intentions-gone-wrong would invade that inspection for planting certified grape vines. The brownie bearer was amiable, and the inspection had proceeded swimmingly and, though I could not have foreseen it then, was doomed. All conditions met and all forms completed, it would have been a success if I had just left it at that...if I had just left it well enough alone. But I wanted to express my gratitude for the courtesy and for the brownies. A newly corked half bottle caught my eye. It was a Zinfandel Port that I was experimenting with. I had racked about ten gallons into carboys and there was just enough left to fill the small bottle, which I had corked. The Port had shown promise at the racking--It was sweet! So, in return for the brownies, I offered him the bottle, which he declined for reasons of propriety on the job. Still within the spirit of returning the good will, I offered him a tasting...as a sample of the wines I hoped to be producing.

The inspector was reluctant to sample it, being on the job (he had several other inspections scheduled and he just couldn't be drinking wine at each, nor even hinting of it). But he allowed that a small "taste" would be considered appropriate within the dictates of his official capacity. This, after all, was the wine business. Glad for the chance to extend my hospitality, I pulled down two Port glasses and proceeded to drive the corkscrew into the new cork. I was excited to try it myself, and it was my first official assignment as house sommelier.

The cork broke in half, of course, but undaunted I got a good start on the remaining plug and got enough of a bite to deftly remove the remainder. Neither of us was prepared for the comedy that was about to reign...or rain. Evidently the Port had not completely finished fermenting. The yeast had busily continued to convert the sugars to alcohol, and also carbon dioxide. As the last millimeter of cork passed the lip of the bottle, it was followed by a geyser of purple, sweet wine. I have ten-foot ceilings, open beams, and two ceiling fans in the kitchen. The ersatz fire extinguisher/fountain showered both fans and all of the ceilings and beams between. That little bottle continued to spray for a seeming infinity, befitting a circus clown's trick bottle. There was just no way that there could have been that much wine in that little container. And as a cascade continued to flow into the sink, wine dripped from beams, fans--and the cap brim, forehead, and chin of the inspector. So much for good intentions. But it doesn't keep you from trying. And I guess it could have been worse: he could have taken the bottle home to the brownie baker.

Chapter 15

The first time I ate organic whole-grain bread I swear it tasted like roofing material.

--Robin Williams

If you can't dazzle them with brilliance, baffle them with bull.

--W. C. Fields

The decision to adhere to organic practices in the vineyard grew out of the "everything you say and do" rule. I had a great respect for the land that I was planting and didn't want to do anything detrimental to it. As the grape planting was being expanded into an additional two acres, I became more cautious. The added stress to the vines, I hoped, would also be beneficial to the wine. In fact I didn't use any fertilizers at all, or herbicides. And the pesticides I used (only one year) were all organic approved.

I understood that the vines could be coaxed into earlier and more rapid first production with fertilizers and insecticides and herbicides. And I saw how not using them had resulted in slower growth, a longer time before first crop, and probably a reduced yield. An acquaintance who worked at a commercial vineyard, a "Mr. Grapevine" with a degree in agriculture, had a much more luxurious growth after three years. I remembered what those winemakers who I respected said about pretty vines not necessarily making pretty wines and endured the ringing superiority of instruction on how to grow grapes..."properly."

I listened to such instructions and did benefit from them. I learned that the "white flies" were leaf hoppers. They were potentially detrimental, destructive even, but I stopped hearing when the inclusion of inorganic pesticides was dictated. And when one Mr. Grapevine started to tell me about something he was using against rodents that might be illegal, I told him that I didn't want to know any more. I didn't want to be put into a position of having to testify against him in court, or being suspected of turning him in if he got caught, or being somehow accused of a contributing role because I did know and didn't turn him in.

The use and banning of DDT had taken place in my generation. And with such horror stories as thalidomide in medicine, I have an informed skepticism of technology when it came to chemistry. There just was no reason to bend to expediency when considering my responsibility toward the land.

It's a funny thing, but it is illegal to say you are organic unless you have been *certified* organic. The fee is nominal and from what I understand, the test is not too rigorous. I have yet to be certified. As I understand it, all you have to do is say that you haven't used any inorganics for three years, and someone comes out to survey (oh good, another invasive inspection), and you are organic. Without the certification, you are forbidden by law from using the term "organic" anywhere in advertising or on the label. It is just another case of a law that makes it harder for those who comply rather than prevent the abuse of the term.

Probably the most persuasive argument against certification came ultimately from the one who had started to tell me about his rodent program. "Yeah, I've been thinking about getting certified, too," he told me. "All's you have to do is say you haven't used anything for three years."

I thought about my vines with a great hallow, sad affection. I sure made them work a lot harder and they sure weren't as pretty as those luxuriant rows on steroids (mentioned here facetiously but perhaps aptly). Ultimately, I just didn't want to be a member of a club where the membership requirements were so abused, no matter how well qualified my vines were. But of even greater concern is having the vehicles of inspectors who have driven in other vineyards--potentially diseased vineyards--bring in diseases either on their tires or the soles of their feet. This risk isn't offset by an organic label on wine that probably doesn't have the impact it does on a head of lettuce or box of strawberries anyway.

But then my sanity has also not been certified. As cuttings were awaited from UC Davis, Doug Waters was called in with his trencher, and plans for a major expansion were undertaken. Oh, what an unfortunate choice of words.

Chapter 16

A Message from Mars

Wine makes a man more pleased with himself; I do not say it makes him more pleasing to others.

--Samuel Johnson, April 28, 1778

As I unwrapped the Three Musketeers candy bar, I noticed with some curiosity that there was printing on the inside of the wrapper. The outside wrapper has changed dozens of times since my grandfather introduced me to the confection a half century ago at Grossheims Corner Grocery, across the street from his house. It cost a nickel then and was segmented into three ridges (to be shared with two friends or one little sister: one for me, one for you, one for me).

Then the outside wrapper had a drawing of the Alexandre Dumas characters. There is no drawing on the outside anymore. It has been replaced by a banner proclaiming "45% less FAT." But in all the years that I have savored the "whipped up, fluffy chocolate-on-chocolate taste" I had never seen writing on the inside. Perhaps it was a sign, a sort of message in a bottle...or a fortune, like those Chinese cookies. It said: "*YOU ARE NOT A WINNER.*"

Kinda discordant, I thought. I didn't care how delicious it was: Just who did this candy bar think it was delivering such a message to? Someone who had just paid seventy-five cents for the pleasure?

On second bite, I calmed. Whipped up fluffy chocolate on chocolate can do that to you. As I was contemplating a major expansion of my planting, it did seem as though the wrapper message might be celestially timed. Perhaps I should give it more thought. I had to admit there was also a grain of truth in the words. I really hadn't won the gold ring. But on the other hand, I hadn't fallen off the carousel either. In fact, the ride had been pretty extraordinary. It would be ungracious to be anything but thankful for the experiences that this life has afforded.

Maybe I hadn't won the Nobel for literature, but I had at least been afforded the privilege of pursuing my life passions. I was writing the manuscript that would become *WALDO*, and I had built a house that I had designed myself. Though it would remain unpainted on the inside and uncarpeted for several more years (through the present actually), because a new passion had been allowed to enter my life: the planting and growing of wine grapes. Like the others, there was hard work involved...a lot of it...and also a sense of achievement: whether the first buds of a newly rooted cutting, or those of a plant a year old emerging from a grow tube, or the first fruit and subsequent harvest.

Also there was the special gratification of producing the end product that is different from any other kind of agriculture. I had grown orchard fruit: plums and peaches and apples. I had grown my own vegetables, and even the herbs to enhance them. But the production of wine is a special activity like no other.

First, in all humility I readily admit that I do not, have not, and never will--not ever--actually make wine. No human has. I do organize it, though. I can cultivate the vines, nurture them through harvest, crush the grapes, press the juice, and eventually bottle the result. But I don't make any of it. I am reminded of the tale about the arrogant genetic scientist who went to God with the proclamation that he could create life. God listened patiently as the scientist boasted and brayed. He said to God, "Just give me a couple of scoops of dirt, and I will make life from it."

"Uh, uh," God replied. "Get your own dirt."

I do not make grapes, nor yeast. I do help them get together, though. But certainly I don't take all of the credit for the results when it comes out well. Not that it always did, especially in the first years. But then it was even more important to learn what went wrong so that you poured less down the sink. Also the emphasis wasn't on making wine those first few years but on the growing of the grapes. I believed that was where the wine was really made, and there was enough retained of the first bottlings to suggest that I was on the right track. It wasn't vintage stuff, but it showed enough fruit, tannins, and acid to be encouraging.

I wanted to sell grapes and thought it was time to test the market. And considering my small production, the home winemaker seemed an ideal target. Some flyers were printed up and distributed among the local wine-making supply stores. The response encouraged the planned extensions of the vineyard.

But the grape sales were to get an unlikely boost from an even more unlikely set of circumstances that also involved the most unlikely assistance...from my dogs. One of the greatest of life's lessons that I have learned, or am still learning, is that when a setback occurs--when something bad happens--it is often a precursor of something good happening that wouldn't have come about any other way. If ever there was such a case, it came at the time that Doug Waters headed down the hill with his trencher to begin the largest so far of the vineyard expansions.

I had returned to the house to feed the dogs. The morning feeding is customarily met with idiotic enthusiasm by all three dogs. There is a lot of jumping around and celebration with ears flapping like the cartoon character Snoopy. Picture Daffy Duck with a hot foot, multiply it by three, and you get a portrait of feeding time for three Labrador retrievers. As I bent down to present Sartre, aka Farfo, with his bowl, he had one more leap that connected squarely with the ubiquitous smoldering briar that dangled from the corner of my mouth. I am a pipe smoker and have been since college. I would regret it that morning as Farf knocked it out of my mouth, sending it across the mudroom, sparks and ash flying, along with part of one of my teeth.

As a boy, I lost a couple of teeth when the front wheel of my bicycle fell off. The bike stopped and I didn't as the handlebars punched a hole in my smile. I knew from experience as I picked up my pipe and tooth that this was not a good thing. Memories of root canals and temporary fittings were relived. Now the reader might wonder how this event, perhaps a case in support of the message from the Three Musketeers, might have anything to do with becoming a winery.

As it turns out, the owner of the lab that would make my new tooth, a dental sculptor, would provide the answer. Joseph Kovacs was an Olympic athlete in his youth in his native Hungary. While representing his country, he defected, coming to the United States without the ability to even speak English. When I met him, he hardly had an accent and had developed a prestigious business. His clients included those with the last name of Mondavi. This might have been enough of a recommendation by itself, but he also had a great enthusiasm for wine and wine making that was no less than my own. Our first conversation was more about grapes, vines, and wine than teeth. I learned that he comes from several generations of winemakers and grape growers. And that the vineyards had been confiscated by the Communists.

I did get an excellent tooth replacement and at a substantial savings. He took payment in several hundred pounds of my second crop, becoming then my biggest customer. And when he came out to collect on my smile, he was like a kid returned to his favorite playground.

He didn't seem to mind that the vines weren't the picture of perfection; it was the fruit that he was interested in. He was also of the school that believed that the vineyard is where the wine making begins. I watched with amusement as he selected samples from the different rows to taste, rolling the fruit over his tongue before crushing it. "What's this one?" he asked, stopping at the half row of Malvasia Bianca. He didn't recognize it by that name. Undoubtedly all varieties have their Hungarian translation. His eyes seemed to recede in concentration, and then brightened, and perhaps it was my imagination but I thought I detected a tear as he nodded in recognition. "My grandfather had this one," he pronounced. I could only guess at the memories evoked, and was glad that I had facilitated them. His knowledge and enthusiasm for my grapes lent valuable moral support to the expansion project that I was embarking on.

Though as Doug Waters completed a trench nearly to my far property line, nearly a half mile long, it would soon seem that I was destined to lend more support to that Three Musketeers pronouncement.

Chapter 17

The first mistake in public business is the going into it.

--Benjamin Franklin

Do not fear mistakes. You will know failure. Continue to reach out.

--Benjamin Franklin

W hile I didn't know it then, I was about to embark on an episode that, seemingly based in sound reasoning, would qualify for a special award for doing dumb things. As Doug Waters disked the whole area intended for planting, I put in nearly a mile of PVC pipe and manifolds. There are, of course, contractors who specialize in this. And they all drive brand-new trucks that cost more than some houses. I wasn't interested in buying someone a new truck or a vacation home. Instead, I purchased my own new car.

This was the first new car I had ever owned. (My wife always got the new ones when I was married.) It wasn't a three-axle behemoth like the irrigation contractors drove. It was a little Subaru Forester. And for all the world, that little car has earned more respect and affection than any Hummer ever could. It has performed every task I have ever asked of it. I loaded a ton of books in it when *WALDO* arrived in Salinas. It was my workhorse in the field, and in the process is has gained a few battle scars. There is a small dent in the front fender where Benito Dusi hitched a ride on a return visit. There is another in the hatch door where I backed into a post at the irrigation supply yard. When someone there commented on the obvious need for a wash, I just explained that I grow grapes and enjoy the process so much that I like to take a little of the vineyard everywhere I go. When unloaded it is almost as much fun to drive as a Porsche. That purchase was no mistake. But my luck has never been inexhaustible.

Irrigation line installation is not rocket science, and although my only previous experience had been the smaller area near the house, I felt capable of doing it myself. There are all kinds of flow-rate data available, and I calculated that one-and-a-half inch manifolds coming off the two-inch main would be able to supply 1,500 plants or about one and three-fourths acres. Six of these manifolds were installed. The suppliers of those pipes were also available to answer questions, and, as a journalist, I thought I was well qualified to ask them. But they were also not rocket scientists, and there was not a small element of hope involved in the installation of the lines. I was counting on gravity flow from the existing water tank to supply pressure, again using the past experience in the original planting, I thought, and had non–rocket scientist support that there would be sufficient water pressure. But until the valves were opened, I just didn't know.

The first planting scheduled was for nearly an acre of Zin. I returned to those wineries and vineyards I respected for more cuttings. Benito Dusi allowed me to select and harvest my own. For the first time I called in outside help, through a farm labor contractor, to lay out the drip lines and assist with the planting. Eight lines, over almost an acre, were installed, running in two separate manifold blocks governed by two valves that controlled four lines each.

On the first test of the first four lines, there was so much pressure that a few emitters were blown out of the hoses. There was enough pressure. And when I opened the second valve, the eight lines reduced the pressure sufficiently that the emitters at least stayed put and life-giving water bubbled forth, creating two-foot-wide wet patches around each prospective planting site.

The satisfaction of seeing it all come together with an acre of dark wet spots was immeasurable. But one can accommodate just so much good fortune. Can't you just hear the bomb ticking?

It was drizzling when the field-workers showed up the next morning. The steel-gray clouds provided a welcome additional amount of water, creating an even more hospitable home for my new cuttings. My plan here was to plant unrooted cuttings...sticks of viable vines of five buds each. There is precedence for this, and I was on a roll, with the irrigation and car purchase. Optimism abounded. This was reinforced by the man in charge. He was not tall, but he had an athletic stride. His confident bearing and dedication to purpose supported trust and commanded respect. There was also something of a rogue about him, too. His name was Miguel and he was thoroughly likeable, one that you would want to be on the same side of in a fight and would trust your vineyard to...if not your sister.

Miguel handled a shovel with dexterity and precision. The shovel wasn't of the ordinary garden, round-pointed variety that I had used. It had a longer, narrow blade and shorter handle, a drain spade. He thrust it into the ground with precision, slicing into the soil with a hiss, maybe using his foot on the top of the blade for one more thrust so that about two-thirds of it was in the ground. Then he worked the handle back and forth against the flat of the blade, opening a slit in the earth. In a continuous fluid motion he dropped a cutting into the slit and then stepped on the loosened ground once or twice, packing the soil back around the dormant stick. The efficiency and economy of movement were entertainment to one who had "dug holes" and then refilled them around the planting. His method was five times more efficient than mine. Grace and virtuosity are not limited to the performing arts.

Since these were being planted before rooting, the grow tubes were filled with moist soil to the top of the cutting to better insulate them and help in retaining moisture. Within two days, there were eight new rows of Zinfandel in the ground.

As a boy, we had spent the summers in Baja. The Mexican culture and cuisine was and is a part of my heritage, though my ancestry is European. When I travel out of the country for extended periods, I have "care packages" of tortillas and cans of refried beans sent. I had studied Spanish in college and lived in Spain and traveled in South and Central America, so I was able to talk with the guys working on my land. I gained new respect for them as I staggered home at the end of the day after trying futilely to keep up with them in the fields. They earned their money. I was thankful for their contribution. They also laughed at my jokes in their language, for which I was even more thankful. It was a festive, joyful experience. My gratitude distilled into respect.

For additional clones of Sangiovese I turned to one of my favorite wineries in the Paso Robles area, Fratelli Perata. The brothers Perata come from a family of Italian winemakers. Their Sangiovese grapes come from vineyards in Montalcino, where they make Brunello, which is probably the quintessential wine of Italy. Though prevented by appellation restrictions from being called Brunello if grown outside Montalcino, the royalty is reflected in the California version. Deep in color, acidic, big fruit from start to finish, the best Sangio I have ever sampled from this side of the Atlantic Ocean.

The Peratas generously allowed me to come in and collect cuttings not only of the Sangio but also of their Nebbiolo. While it comes from the cooler, northern regions of Italy, where the Barolo and Barbaresco vie for national supremacy with the Tuscan varieties, the wines produced in the Paso Robles area from the grape offered promise enough to justify a few trial rows. Lighter and smoother than the Sangio, I envisioned a natural expansion of the varieties the Volo Del Corvo ranch might offer.

Within a couple of days, the field-workers had these in the ground. The lower vineyard had just over an acre of grow tubes--neat salmon-colored rows. On the last day, I paid them in cash with a little extra--the equivalent of a couple of hours of work, which didn't begin to convey my appreciation. In addition, also with the intent of extending my gratitude, I gave each worker a few packages of frozen steaks from a wild boar that I had shot. I think they were a little puzzled by the gesture.

As they left, I felt a bittersweet sense of accomplishment. The fields that had brimmed with activity and conversation in Spanish lay silent and still.

The silence didn't extend to the mudroom of the house, however. The three Labs greeted me with their typical enthusiasm of idiots, also making it known that it was supper time for them.

After speaking only Spanish for several days, I found myself commanding the dogs to "Siéntese" (sit). Remarkably, they obeyed.

As I began to remove the muddy clothes in preparation for a much-needed shower (the dogs told me), I set the contents of my pockets on the counter in the laundry room: a knife, a drip-line punch, and some drip emitters. The Spanish word for the emitters is "guatero." I didn't know it then as I surveyed the deceptively tranquil new addition to the vineyard nearly a quarter of a mile away, but this was the calm before the storm. As I put my version of enchiladas into the oven, savoring the mixed feelings of fatigue, satisfaction, and gratitude, I didn't envision that I had just left a battlefield.

Chapter 18

The Boar Wars

Italians come to ruin most generally in three ways, women, gambling, and farming. My family chose the slowest one.
--Pope John XXIII

The next morning there was a slight drizzle-mist-fog that is common here in early Spring. I thought I would start the irrigation on the newly planted vine rows anyway. There were five areas planted all on different valves. Each had four rows. Starting with the first vines planted, from the old-vine Dusi Zin, the first valve was opened. There was a lag as the drip lines refilled. And as they did, a spout of water issued from a missing emitter, then another...and another, a dozen in all. My first thought was that there was too much pressure for the four lines and I was blowing the emitters.

I tried the second valve...same problem, though less than twelve were blown there. Slightly fewer emitters blew on the other three groups, but probably a total of forty in all.

I closed all of the valves, stuffed my pocket with new emitters, and set out to replace the missing ones in the first two groups. Eight lines of forty-four plants, the total length was nearly three-fifth of a mile. It took just over an hour. I noticed a few animal tracks but didn't think much about it at the time. They were cloven hooves...deer and wild pigs. The arrow-head-shaped ones were deer, the wider, larger ones, pigs.

When I tried the water again, the first valve was only opened halfway and a second was opened fully after which the first was fully opened. No emitters were blown. Agua trickled out of three hundred and fifty guateros. Little dark spots began to spread around each grow tube. As the drip lines were still on the ground (later they would be suspended from a wire running the length of the row), a second hour was spent adjusting the placement so that the water most benefited the individual plants. In some places a second emitter had to be inserted further uphill. If these cuttings were going to sprout, the success depended on a reliable water source. The ground around each had to be kept damp.

I thought the problem of blowing emitters was solved. By opening two valves at a time, the pressure was more evenly distributed and the emitters stayed in the tubes. However, the plastic drip line expands and contracts with temperature change. The cold nights, which were still in the forties and high thirties, shrank the tubes. Each day the lines had to be readjusted. Each emitter had to be checked to see that the plant was getting the required water. The water from each eventually spreads out to a diameter of up to four feet below the surface, but with the plants still forming roots, there had to be a little more precision on top.

Then about the third day, a whole lot of emitters were blown again. It wasn't water pressure doing it, it was the wildlife. The deer and also the wild pigs were coming in at night, pulling off the guateros and helping themselves to the trickle of water. Something was also gnawing holes in the lines themselves. These had to be patched by cutting the line and inserting a connector wherever there was a hole. This added immeasurably to the pleasure of my days...or at least to half of them. As the days progressed, I would replace as many as one hundred emitters in a single morning. Bambi and Porky were not my favorite cartoon characters.

After several days, I began selecting a few plants at random to get a peek at the success. The buds were swelling, several had even leafed out. Hope! On those that hadn't leafed, I cut a little notch at the top to verify that the cutting was still green. They were. More hope!

Then the weather changed, spring was in full gear and the promise of summer with the thermometer in the eighties. While the pigs and deer became less frequent, the ground was drying out quicker and water had to be applied twice a day. Some of the plants that had sprouted leaves withered.

Three weeks went by in which most of my days were spent tending the new planting. I thought it was time to remove the dirt from the cones. Judging from the peeking, less than a third of the cuttings had survived. There was the hope that deeper down the vines had rooted and were growing. I could only control the water and had spent the better part of almost three weeks seeing to it that each plant got the maximum I could get to it.

Starting at the top of the hill, I started lifting cones and removing the dirt from around the cuttings. The results were not good...terrible. The first twenty produced only a couple that even showed the hope of still being alive. One had leaves...one plant out of twenty. As you go further down the hill, the soil is richer. Not rich, just less rocky. The grasses around the cones were more luxuriant. "Maybe I should grow hay," I thought.

Actually, the first year that I lived here, I had leased out the land on speculation to a barley farmer. Barley is a common crop in the area, used for hay. Cliff Plaskett was descended from several generations of local people and had been farming all of his life. He and his sons owned several times the acreage that I had. They had all of the heavy machinery to do the job right, yet because it was a dry year, only a trace of stubble, nothing harvestable, was produced. It was a disappointment. But not anywhere near the dismal dejection experienced at finding dead stick after dead stick where there had been such high hopes just weeks before. The expense of hiring the workers, the work expended in planting and even more in keeping the irrigation going were wasted. The plan just didn't work. I was reminded of Cliff's response to the failed barley crop. He was one of the most generous men I have ever known...generous in his actions toward others. There was one local individual who had dished him some dirt. But rather than be vindictive, he just refused to comment. "I have just learned that it does no good to speak ill of another," he would say.

When I was building my house, Cliff was fighting his final bout with cancer. My newly constructed basement had flooded without any cover that first year. Once, when I came up from Los Angeles to work, I found a mallard duck paddling around in it. Cliff showed up with an industrial strength pump when he got word of my plight. It was a heavy piece of equipment even for a young man, yet he refused help dropping it into place. "I guess I'm not much good anymore," he apologized. The irony was that he couldn't have been more help or have done better. Water poured out of the basement like out of a fire hose. When his crop of barley failed, he had been hoping for some good result to defray some of his medical bills. I was reminded of his response as I looked over the bleak results of my most recent planting. His health was failing, he had just invested in seed and diesel fuel and a lot of time in planting barley, yet there wasn't an ounce of defeat in his demeanor. He just looked me in the eye with determined courage and acceptance. "That's farming," he shrugged.

I can't pretend to that level of magnanimity with my recent effort, but the memory did help. It was a pretty tough act to follow. That was his last year on earth. His nature came from a life of boom-and-bust experiences. I was just getting started by comparison. This was just my round one. And as I came up from the canvas, some of the experience would come in handy as I was about to nearly get Doug Waters electrocuted.

Chapter 19

Laughter is the shortest distance between two people.

--Victor Borge

You've got to be very careful if you don't know where you are going, because you might not get there

--Yogi Berra

They say that every success story has behind it the experience of failure. I don't know who "they" are. It would add weight to the theory if "they" were identified and deemed successful. I guess it would probably be accurate to assume that at some time everyone experiences some form of setback. There are probably those who experience failure exclusively. At times it has felt like I could be counted among them. There are others whose success far outshines the antithesis.

I have always been fascinated by those historical figures who were winners on a grand scale, from Alexander the Great to Howard Hughes. And more modern-day ones, like the comedian Jim Carey, who recounts that early in his career he drove up to the hills above Hollywood and, looking down, vowed that he would make it there someday. Or more locally, Clint Eastwood, whose influence goes back to my induction into the army during the Vietnam War.

Being drafted was not the favorite time of my life. It was far too much like being in prison; it was certainly not one of my successes. During basic training at Ford Ord we were confined to the barracks. On the few forays to the PX we were marched there under the supervision of the drill sergeant. We couldn't even buy toothpaste on our own. Ten weeks later, it was more of the same at Fort Sam Houston in Texas. It wasn't until we were in advanced training as surgical technicians that we got to go off the post, nearly five months after first being interned...uh, I mean inducted. Most of us had come from California and for our first celebration we chose a Mexican restaurant for lunch. Afterward, sated and slightly tipsy on remarkably little beer (not having had any for almost half a year), we drifted into a local theater where *A Fistful of Dollars* and *For a Few Dollars More* were playing.

I had not been that familiar with the work of Mr. Eastwood at that time, but that evening as we strolled back to our cells...uh, barracks...it was with a renewed cheer. The escape and entertainment so contrasted with the previous half year of indoctrination. There was the feeling of just being alive again, and that somehow this time would be survived. I have ever since been indebted to "The Man with No Name" as he built a legendary one in the movie industry. His movies had provided counterpoint to a very depressing time in my life.

Living just over an hour away from Carmel, where he presided as mayor at the time I bought my ranch, I have had a special interest in his diverse career. I have yet to meet someone who has known him that has anything but compliments. On what might be counted as one of my short, but not unsuccessful, dating ventures, the lady in question had worked for him.

One evening as we drove to his excellent restaurant, which has a commanding view of the Carmel River emptying into the Pacific, the man was standing in the parking lot. My date waved as we parked. As he called a greeting to her, I realized I was about to get a formal introduction to someone I held in great esteem, a hero from my army days.

"Mr. Eastwood, it's good to see you," I said as my date made the introduction.

"You can call me Clint," he corrected. "It's good to see you, too," he said. I was impressed by his warmth and also the size of his hand as we shook hands. I wanted to say something witty and wanted to recount the uplifting effect his movies had that is recalled above. When my date invited him to join us later inside (he was on his way out), I remembered a saying about treating regular people like celebrities and treating celebrities like regular people. Inspired by that and also by his genuineness (he said to call him Clint, after all), I quipped, "If you come back, I'll buy you one of those watered-down drinks they serve in this place [his restaurant]."

In all of my memories of Clint Eastwood movies, I cannot ever remember hearing him laugh. It was a youthful, from-the-belly laugh. He turned, "I'll take the water part," he said, grinning.

He didn't come back, but my meal, which would have been savored on its own merits, was even more memorable with the knowledge that I had just made Clint Eastwood laugh. I didn't get to thank him for the uplifting years before, but in some small way I had partially paid him back.

I got to thinking later about that regular people and celebrity saying. I thought about Cliff Plaskett, wracked with cancer, and what he did for me that day with the flooded basement--no less of an impact at a different time in my life than those Clint Eastwood movies. I had made Cliff laugh, too. And a couple of times, he did accept the proffered can of beer. I was no less glad for that...and in my mind, no less of a success.

As I thought about it, I noticed they had two things in common. First was generosity: demonstrated by a dying man lending a hand or the pleasure exhibited by Mr. Eastwood when his co-workers get recognition, too. When he won a couple of Academy Awards for *Million Dollar Baby*, his costars also won Oscars. When those awards were announced the cameras panned back to a grin bigger than when he got his own...the same grin won when he told me he would "take the water part."

They also had in common that they didn't seek to make the same mistake twice. Not all of Clint Eastwood's movies have been great successes. When one isn't, he doesn't go out and try to remake it. Cliff Plaskett declined to farm my land again. Barley needed better ground. This would not be a condemnation of my land for wine grapes, however. Remember the old Italian maxim about the poorer the soil, the richer the vine would make you? Mr. Plaskett had in effect pronounced success for the vines.

It was just up to me not to repeat my failures, which, in this case, was planting sticks in the ground. Buying the plants commercially was just too cost prohibitive. I knew I had to get them started first, like I had done with the Dusi and Mondavi vines, in the basement. But the basement capacity was just not adequate. I needed a greenhouse. Why repeat failures, when you can go out and begin a whole set of new ones?

Chapter 20

If I seem to take part in politics, it is only because politics encircles us today like the coil of a snake from which one cannot get out, no matter how much one tries. I wish therefore to wrestle with the snake.
--Mahatma Gandhi

The smallest minority on earth is the individual. Those who deny individual rights cannot claim to be defenders of minorities.
--Ayn Rand

It will probably come as no surprise that there was a roadblock in getting that greenhouse. It should come as less of a wonder that the roadblock would involve government red tape. Since the Spanish padres first colonized the state, the construction of utility buildings had been exempt from building codes. In fact none of the missions had building permits and they have stood for over two hundred years. OK, the earthquakes and wind and rain have taken their tolls on those graceful adobe structures including nearby Mission San Antonio. And it is a good thing that when you buy a house today that there is some standard of reliability, that it won't blow down as you're moving in.

When I built my house, I designed it myself and built it to higher standards than the building codes. It still cost several thousands of dollars to have my plans reviewed and approved: "Yep, that's good enough." About the only problems I had was with some of the fire codes: the #*&% alarm that goes off when I light my pipe. And then there were the windows in one bedroom. When designing the house, I had to keep in mind the maximum allowable glazing area--there is a limit to the square footage of windows to square footage of total building allowed. This is for structural and heating reasons (people can't live in glass houses). The house was approved within two square feet of that maximum. But when I reduced the size of the windows in one bedroom during construction because it offered aesthetic symmetry from the outside, I didn't think there would be a problem as the glazing area was being reduced. But not taken into account was the fact that the smaller windows made it more difficult for a fireman with a backpack to enter.

I promised to never have a fire in that room, but to no avail. I had to call it a sewing room instead of a bedroom. At least they didn't make me show proof of purchase of a sewing machine. And the distance to the floor from the windows in another bedroom was eight inches over the maximum. I had to raise the floor in the room as the windows were already installed. The self-closing steel door to the attached garage was yet another problem. I don't mind the idea of a steel door there, but do mind that Big Brother wants to make sure that you keep it closed and doesn't give you enough credit to be able to do it yourself. You have to block it open when you carry in groceries, and it is almost impossible to bring a ladder into the house via that entry.

Until recently, nearly every barn, stable, and tool shed in the state had been exempt from building codes. They were considered temporary buildings, not for human occupation. That heritage helped build this country. When a farmer needed a structure to house his tools or protect his livestock from the weather, he built one. Greenhouses were included in those temporary structures. Presumably, the farmer or rancher would think enough of his cow or his plow to build a structure strong enough to protect them. Often these structures were built better than the ones the farmers and ranchers lived in.

As I researched greenhouses, subscribing to a variety of catalogues, the standards for building greenhouses were just undergoing evaluation. I wasn't looking to build the National Arboretum, just something that could house a few hundred grapevines out of the late winter and early spring frosts. I found what I thought was an ideal solution. One of the neighboring vineyards had one. It was an inflatable building, two layers of soft pliable plastic that were filled like a giant balloon. In the days before building code requirements, you could install one of these for a fraction of the cost of rigid construction. But since there was no new code covering such a structure in the "new" statutes, a permit to install one could not be issued. Out of luck there.

Structures less than 120 square feet were exempt from the building codes, however. Basically, this is a storage shed...ten feet by twelve feet. It isn't difficult to accumulate a footstool-size stack of catalogues for greenhouses in this size or smaller. Today if you Google on 10 x 12 greenhouses, you get over 1,300 hits. You have a wide choice of materials and vents and accessories.

I wanted to keep it simple. I was also attracted to a rigid plastic glazing with airspace between the two sheets, which added to the insulation as well as the cost. But by building my own, I calculated that I could do it with this insulating property for about the price of a manufactured, single-layer-of-glazing one. For the flooring, I first put down some wire rodent barrier, then just square paving stones. The wall framing was cross-braced with cordon wire with a mid-run tensioner. The rigid plastic glazing was screwed to the frame. A bench was installed at half-height, effectively creating a two-story greenhouse (doubling the planting area).

The door was an easily installed storm door from Sears; the vents and exhaust fan came from Grainger. The new structure was built within extension cord reach of the water holding tank, but the power was brought right to the new greenhouse when Doug Waters, trenching for the expansion of the vineyard, cut through the live power line to the well. I looked up from my greenhouse framing in time to see Doug set a new world record for the combined broad and high jumps as he leapt from his trencher, wires--live wires--flailing from the giant chain boom of the machine. It was my fault; I hadn't marked the run correctly. I did a pretty fair hop, skip, and jump of my own to the nearby electric panel. The circuit breakers, thankfully, had functioned (not all building codes are without merit). Imagining all too clearly the potential disaster that had been averted, I felt a combined relief and remorse as I helped Doug untangle the spaghetti wound around his trencher blade. Catastrophe averted, we returned to our respective endeavors...with one new task on my list: repair the electric connection to the well.

Ultimately, the greenhouse worked great. Within a couple of weeks, I stood in the entry to the little structure, with the benches, and the space under the benches, full of growing plants--even the central floor in the back was full of flats. There was just a little path, so that you could water. You almost expected to hear one of those tropical recordings with the bird calls in the background and the vibraphone toning exotic music. There is no doubt about the satisfaction--the pleasure of creative, constructive endeavors. In my travels I have seen that it is universal, even in the animal world, as dogs lather themselves silly in pursuit of a rodent or in the Galapagos where a finch has taught itself to use small twigs to pry insects out of tree bark. The satisfaction of constructive activities is not all-inclusive, however, as events would soon verify on several levels.

Chapter 21

2001: The Year of the Snake

The year began with great promise. Rain. Lots of it. In wet years, a creek runs down through my ranch along the edge of the lower vineyard. Free water, I usually say. It was ideal weather for staying in and putting the finishing touches on *WALDO*. It was probably propitious, but the story is about moving to the country, building a house, and the suspected plagiarism of a manuscript I had written a decade before, a novel about the Japanese Americans before, during, and after World War II. The book began with the day Pearl Harbor was attacked in 1941. That year was also a Year of the Snake.

Before moving to the country, I was not nearly as open-minded about intellectual/spiritual pursuits such as astrology, or about the Chinese versions, which are annually based on one of twelve animals. A person born during a given year is supposed to be disposed to certain traits (mostly positive) of the animal in question. Western culture ascribes more negative connotations to some of these animals than the Chinese do.

I was born in the Year of the Dog. Being a great dog lover, that doesn't seem too bad of an assignment. I admire my dogs and in *Waldo* I describe how I tried to assume his best trait of gentleness. The Chinese also attribute to the dog loyalty, honesty, friendliness, reliability, and discretion. In addition, they attribute some negative qualities that sound like messages from the inside of candy bar wrappers, in line with things that my ex said about me. But then she also said that I was the son-of-a-one...and she was Chinese (actually she still is).

Living in the country, I do the kind of work that some say Americans don't do any more. ("There is no such thing as a lousy job; only lousy men who don't want to do them," Ayn Rand.) It gives one so inclined the time to think. Not that all who do this kind of work are so inclined. It does seem that many consider *thinking* a subset of lousy work. It is certainly out of fashion.

Country living certainly allows for the opening of one's mind. My mind may not have any more in it than before, but it is at least open to the possibility. If you were to say that you had seen a flying saucer, I would "now" be open to the prospect. If you were to say there was one in your backyard next door, I would be willing to go over to see it. If you lived much farther away, I might not. If you were to invite me to go for a ride in one, I would decline. Alien drivers do not have the best reputation. Besides, I have too much to do on this planet for one lifetime.

From an intellectual standpoint, I am open the possibility that the conditions of the universe at the time of birth might have some influence on one's nature. I am not drawn to the fortune-telling aspect of astrology, but I do find it an interesting intellectual pursuit. This came through the works of Carl Jung, the psychologist, whose pioneering in personality typing led to tests such as the Meyers-Briggs, which is widely accepted throughout science and industry and the military. These works were of particular interest to a writer wanting to put depth into his fictional characters. If I could give them a type, all kinds of interesting traits could be built around them. Jung also believed that astrology as seen in birth charts has an influence on the typing.

Not intending to make this chapter an apology for astrology, I have noticed some correlation with the ancient science and dating. Solitude and privacy does not mean isolation. While living in a rural area does cut down on the "walk-in traffic," the Internet has more than made up for it. Only two ladies have ever come to my front door unannounced in a decade of living here. One was a sheriff (not looking for me) and the other was selling the *Watchtower*. However, through the miracle of the Internet, it has been possible to keep some semblance of social contact with the known world. At times my fortunes seem to fly in the face of that pronouncement on the inside of the Three Musketeers wrapper. Notables were a former movie star and Playboy model, and as if to atone for the Miss America blunder, another who had been named "Miss Congeniality" in a different year of the Miss America Pageant. Suffice to say, while that relationship was not one meant to be, as a gentleman I would never contest the appropriateness of her award.

I can tell you, too, that I have noticed a certain pattern of compatibilities with astrological signs. And also that there are some who have noticed incompatibilities where I hadn't. Oh well, I just remain thankful for the successes and maintain the philosophy that it is better to have loved than to have lost.

The Year of the Snake started out to be an exercise without an Eve although it promised to be a good growing year in Eden. Except that the last ten vines of each row in the lower, new vineyard were almost in a swamp. As I surveyed the potential damage, I had no idea what the excess water would do to them. I hoped, correctly as it turned out, that their dormancy would protect them. And as spring floods were followed by a run of sun, I found I needed to put in valves in each row at the lower, sloggy ends to cut off irrigation, as the higher vines started to clamor for water.

It seemed to take forever for the swamps to dry out, but as they did so, I was rewarded by budding branches. And by the time it was dry enough to drive down there, the extra water seemed to have benefited the vines at the lower end as they leafed out luxuriantly. It wasn't long before I was opening the valves to those vines. And after several weeks of what seemed unwarranted worry, it did seem that a feared drowning and catastrophe had been averted.

But true to country living, just as you eliminate one worry, something else comes up to replace it. As I was checking the flow from the newly resupplied lower emitters one evening, I noticed several spots where some tiny insects were swarming. They weren't ants, though they were about that size. On several occasions in previous years I had noted some sort of mite. These had never done any damage, and as it was getting dark, I really couldn't tell what these were or the extent of their population. I just resolved to not let a new worry ruin the relief of having overcome one now vanquished concern. What's the saying about ignorance being bliss?

Chapter 22

The Battle of Britain

We shall fight on the beaches, we shall
fight on the landing-grounds, we shall fight
in the fields...
--Winston Churchill

Several months before, an alert had been issued to vineyards throughout the state to watch for the glassy-winged sharpshooter. The insect is the vehicle for the dreaded Pierce's disease, a bacterial infection that is particularly lethal to grapevines. The bacteria that causes the disease is *Xylella fastidiosa.* It has wiped out whole vineyards. It has resulted also in severe restrictions on grapevine transfer throughout the state. Today, I probably would not be able to receive the cuttings that are now planted in my vineyard.

To say the least, I had been on the lookout for the beast, and alert to the possibility that the bugs I had seen were sharpshooters. But when I went down the next day, the swarms I had seen the previous evening were gone. One of the things you learn about living in the country is that some problems do just go away. I mentioned that I had noticed small swarms of insects in previous years, probably gnats or some sorts of mites. And they just went away on their own.

That isn't always the final solution, but if the problem goes away, there is nothing to fix. And with a to-do-list that grows on its own, you don't go around looking for new additions. The house that had been "finished" four years before still needed cabinets and window trim and was still without carpeting. So some phantom bugs got a low priority.

In this case, though, it was a mistake. The reason I didn't see any bugs the second day was that I went out at midday and it was warm. The bugs had retreated into the grass, out of sight. Several days later, as I was again irrigating the spot where I first had noticed them, they were back. Not in as great numbers (infant mortality) but enough to get one's attention. And they were larger and had attained a more identifiable form...miniatures of their adult shape. They were not sharpshooters. They were grasshoppers.

I really didn't know what kind of a problem I was in for. I had no inkling of the potential harm they could inflict. Sure I knew of the story of the locusts in Utah and the statue of the Seagull dedicated to the flocks that had saved the Mormon settlers' crops. It is part of American folklore. Any numbers of sprays were available but they would violate the standards of caring for the land that I had committed to. The battle that was about to be waged would drive me to the brink of being committed...to a mental institution.

As a journalist, I have learned how to identify what I don't know and what I need to know. And how to get that knowledge. Given a good library and a good librarian, a good journalist can become the second greatest expert on any given subject. The greatest experts are those who had written the books.

The Internet has made that job easier. Not only does it give you the information, it gives you the e-mail addresses and other contact information for the experts. I was soon talking to grasshopper entomologists throughout the United States. I learned heaps. And some of the information wasn't encouraging. Grasshoppers are tough. When they are young, they are most vulnerable, but as they progress through their molts, they become almost armor plated. As most of the research grants are related to the pesticide industry, I got a lot of recommendations for inorganic insecticides, but I dismissed them respectfully. From one organic source, I got the suggestion to try neem oil.

Some quick research made it appealing. Derived from the seeds of a plant that grows in Asia, *Azadirachta indica*, the oil is harmless to animals and birds and can cause grief to some insects. What would it do to grasshoppers? I didn't know.

Suited up with a backpack spray unit filled with a properly diluted solution of the oil, I walked out to where the bugs were the thickest--Luke Skywalker against the storm-trooper battalions. By now some had grown enough to start climbing up the vines. They scattered as the exotic artillery was unleashed: The Force be with you. Driving the enemy to retreat held some satisfaction. Many of the vines still had grow tubes and I shot a volley down into the middle of each.

Combat was again waged in the afternoon--the *Millennium Falcon* returns. I envisioned an insect version of the carnage scene from *The Godfather*. This time the bugs held a little more resolutely. I didn't know if they were reinforcements or if the spray was failing. It turned out to be both. After three days, I gave up on neem oil. Plain water did as well. It drove them off, but within minutes, the branches were reinfiltrated--seemingly twofold. They had shields--chitin, the same as lobsters--that no light saber could dent.

Outside of my first days as a draftee in the army, this was the most dismal time of my life. They lined up on the most mature branches almost like railroad cars on a long freight train, from trunk to the tip of every branch, devouring everything green. The grow tubes did nothing to protect the plants inside. I even went to a yardage shop and bought a few yards of that mesh that ballerina tutus are made from (now that got some looks). Hans Solo would never have done this, but I just wanted to do everything I could. I cut this into squares and paper clipped them over the tops of the tubes. For some, this worked; for others it was too late--the young vines were eaten to the ground.

You could lift a tube and grasshoppers would pour out of the bottom. You could grab a branch of a more mature plant and strip them off like rosemary leaves. I was exhausted from frustration, which hit a peak when I yanked a two-year-old vine lined with grasshoppers out of the ground and beat it and them on the earth in rage.

The radio news syndicates had been alerted of my plight and I was called for interviews. The Volo Del Corvo was news. I tried to put on the bold face, wondering if this is how farmers in the dust bowl had felt decades before. Even television picked up on the story. The local NBC affiliate sent out a crew to document the disaster.

A funny thing, it was the second time in as many weeks that I was on television. The first time was for my recently published book, *WALDO*. As it was reviewed gloriously in the local Carmel newspaper and was received warmly in area bookstores, Rick Martel, the vicinal version of Oprah (or, more aptly, Merv Griffin) invited me on-air to tout my publication.

It seemed incongruous that one half of my life was going into the toilet as perhaps the most important aspect showed signs of life. But no matter how great a new pair of shoes might be, if you have a rock in one of them, that gets the attention.

One of the greatest mistakes I had made with respect to dealing with the grasshoppers was to leave the weeds. I had thought that leaving an alternative food source would have been beneficial. Having exhausted everything else I could think of, I once again called on Doug Waters and his tractor disk.

I watched with an almost sadistic glee as he towed his disks between the vine rows, turning over the earth and plowing under the bugs. I imagined the carnage that the steel blades might be wreaking. Remarkably, the stage was set for one of my favorite episodes--certainly one of the most spiritual--experienced on the ranch.

Chapter 23

The Flight of the Crow

I had been giving a lot of thought to the spiritual implications of the grasshopper infestation of my vineyards. Three-year-old vines are stripped of their leaves. Younger vines are cut off at the ground. I went looking for a book on animal symbolism to see what it said about grasshoppers. It is the same book referenced in *WALDO*. The following is an excerpt about that animal symbolism book:

> *Carl Jung's studies of intuition, synchronicity, the subconscious, and dreams are the reasons that I was attracted to his work. While I can't say that I subscribe to everything that he and all of the others have to say about the significance of dreams (you gotta keep the balance), I do try to notice when there is a correlation between dreams and "reality." That correlation was responsible for the naming of my ranch. In my dream, there was a great bird with plumage so shiny and black that it reflected sunlight in little rainbows of color, like oil on water. The huge bird was being handled like a falcon by a man who did not speak. But it wasn't a falcon. When I asked what it was, he remained mute and sent the bird to flight. It flew almost in slow motion, with a massive, undulating wing beat.*
>
> *The next morning, fully awake, Waldo and I were out on our run when we encountered one of*

the largest nonpredatory birds I had ever seen. It was a crow. It was perched on a fence post just outside of the entry gate to the ranch. Waldo, whose breeding has endowed him with a keen interest in fowl, paid absolutely no attention to this one. It was as if he didn't see him.

The bird did not seem to mind us either. It remained on its perch until we were exactly opposite, on the other side of the narrow country road. I stood there fascinated as Waldo proceeded to rummage around in the brush, ignoring it entirely. Wondering just how close I would be permitted to get, I stepped toward it. One step and the bird spread its immense wings and flew away...exactly as the one in my dream had done: almost in slow motion, great undulating wing beats, sun shining off jet feathers that reflected little rainbows of color.

Later in the week, I purchased a volume on animal symbolism. I wanted to read what qualities tradition had assigned to the crow. As I was reading my new purchase, I was distracted by the call of a bird in the trees above me. The cawing made reading nearly impossible.

The crow, I learned, is a symbol of mystery, of the law, and the messenger of truth. I incorporated it into the name of my ranch. Because the climate and terrain reminds me of Tuscany, I chose an Italian translation: Volo Del Corvo, the flight of the crow. Balance dictates that I don't form a religion around the noble bird, only to appreciate it and be fascinated by it when encountered. I take notice with wry joy each time I encounter one. It is almost as if I had been let in on some private mystical secret...or joke.

But the story continues: While attending a meeting of the Central Coast Jung Society, I noticed a small booklet from the C. G. Jung Bookstore in

*Los Angeles. What had attracted me to the book was
the cover illustration: a drawing of a crow. I have
to admit that I was not surprised when I turned to
page twelve and found a review of a book on animal
symbolism, the same one I had bought a couple of
months before when researching the crow. By then,
such occurrences were almost taken for granted.
You do have to laugh. The crow: the messenger, the
law.*

I am, of course, aware of the Old Testament accounts of
locust plagues visited on the people for wrongdoing. The
symbolism book does reference these, but then explains that
most other cultures have a different view of the
grasshopper/cricket (our wonderful guilt legacy!). The
grasshopper is venerated by the rest of the world. It only
goes in a forward direction. It is symbolic of great leaps
forward--accelerated progress. Jeeze, I wish I had been able
to find that book earlier. I had been wondering what I had
done to reap such punishment. I do try to be careful in my
conduct of life not to deserve such rewards and really
couldn't reconcile it. I just thought somehow that the event
could become beneficial eventually.

First, I knew it would make up several chapters in my
next (this) book. So there was that benefit. But I noted that I
also had been getting a lot of publicity. I was on a television
talk show in San Luis Obispo for my book. In addition, I had
been reviewed in two Monterey newspapers. But the bugs
also brought publicity...at least for the vineyard. I was
interviewed for radio by Cal Ag News Byte, the AP, as well
as local newspapers. Then the NBC-TV affiliate came out
and shot a human-interest piece on the bugs. It really turned
out well. I was getting publicity for the book and the
Vineyards. Radio, newspapers, TV...some leap.

The severity of the infestation was compounded because
I was committed to a higher standard of farming, and the
organic stuff doesn't do much against grasshoppers. I had
tried several organic sprays, which the bugs seem to regard

as delicious. Weeding and mowing the groundcover seemed to help (organic farmers don't use herbicides either), so I resolved to do that. I started to go out to weedwhack where Doug's tractor couldn't go. But I stopped halfway down the hill. The vineyards, you see, were full. Not of grasshoppers (oh, they were still there). But also out there: bug-eating...*crows*. A great flock of them.

And again the next day, I couldn't have created a fiction story that better illustrated the phrase, "You can't control the events in your life, but you can control your response to them." I was thankful the stuff I had sprayed was organic. If I had used anything else, the crows would have been poisoned. I have to tell you that it isn't easy to keep to the healthy commitment when your vines are being stripped-- vines that you gathered as cuttings several years before, and rooted in the greenhouse, and planted one at a time in the field. It was a neat message from the Crow.

Chapter 24

According to most studies, people's number one fear is public speaking. Number two is death. Death is number two. Does that sound right? This means to the average person, if you go to a funeral you're better off in the casket than doing the eulogy.

--Jerry Seinfeld

By the time the older vines were ready to pick, the grasshoppers had all but vanished. I had been advised by the entomologists that within seven weeks of the initial infestation, the invaders would run through their life cycle. It was a hellish almost two months. In the end, they never got very bad on the older vines near the house, and with the summer heat through the month of August, the grapes there were ready for harvest.

I have to admit to being a little trigger happy when it comes to harvest. You do want to test several bunches to get a more accurate sampling. I have a propensity for testing the ripest grapes. The darkest in color, they shine with seduction, like the apple in Eden. You can taste it when they are sweet; if you don't have a refractometer, with some practice you can get some idea of the sugar content. Examining the seeds (wine grapes aren't seedless) can also tell you something about the ripeness. If they are still green, you might want to put off harvest.

All of my available grapes were spoken for by home winemakers. Typically a home winemaker uses five-gallon glass carboys for secondary fermentation. You need about one hundred pounds of grapes to make five gallons of wine, which in turn makes about twenty-five bottles. I was charging fifty cents a pound if the winemakers picked themselves. I crushed for them as part of the deal. So, I was selling wine at two dollars a bottle. Sure you need to take into consideration a couple of hours to pick one hundred pounds, a few more to press and rack and finally bottle, and the initial investment for equipment such as the carboy and some food-grade plastic containers (which are reusable year after year). But if the quality is there, it measures out as a pretty good deal for the home winemaker.

But that can be a big *if.* I had poured more than one carboy down the drain. But the results were getting better and better with fewer failures and some noteworthy successes. In an effort to supply the best quality and optimum potential, I kept those who had signed up for grapes informed on the ripening. For one brief moment, there was a respite to enjoy the satisfaction of achievement. As I bottled some not too shabby 2000, with the grasshopper invasion behind me and with many of the stripped vines showing valiant new buds, it was possible to watch with interest the tape of the NBC newscast. I made a tape of it and combined it with the one that reviewed my book.

I was a pretty harsh self-critic but found some pleasure in the rookie on-screen performances. I stumbled when asked to read an excerpt from my book. I don't know how to explain that, but reading out loud from your own work smacks of arrogance. I guess that Rick Martel picked up on that (or maybe I just wasn't good at it), but he read the next selection himself. They were funny excerpts and I appreciated hearing that other people thought they were funny, too. I was also funny on air, when the host produced an orange-scented spray (a sponsor?) and a fine fragrant mist drifted down. "Gee, Rick," I protested. "I did bathe before I came."

OK, so Letterman and Leno don't have any worry, but this was my first on-camera experience. And with no small thanks to Mr. Martel, I enjoyed it.

And as I led the cameras through my vineyard during the invasion, trying to maintain a stiff upper lip when asked about my response to the mess, I had quipped, "There is some language I use off camera, that you wouldn't let me use on." In that bit, the camera panned to the higher, relatively unmolested vineyard, green and lush, with the house I had built, bright white in contrast, with its porches and gables. A decade of my life was captured there. The moisture in the eyes was not a result of irritation from pipe smoke.

In a matter of hours it would happen again. The tears. Tenfold. But not from reruns. 2001 was the Year of the Snake.

Chapter 25

All the great things are simple, and many can be expressed in a single word: freedom, justice, honor, duty, mercy, hope.
--Winston Churchill

The man who trades freedom for security does not deserve nor will he ever receive either.

--Benjamin Franklin

As I waited for the first of the year's customers to come for the first harvest, I was at my computer, working on a sales brochure for *WALDO*. The *Today Show* was on TV. I was a huge Katie Kouric fan. I often have the news program on when I am working at tasks that don't require a great deal of total concentration. There was a late-breaking news bulletin. The big screen behind her was of one of the buildings that made up the World Trade Center. It was from a live television camera. There was smoke billowing as Ms. Kouric described how a jet passenger plane had crashed into it.

My first reaction was to wonder how a pilot could have been so stupid. But as she described it, a second plane came into view from the right and sliced into the second tower in a ball of flames. I am reminded of the closing words of Kurtz in *Apocalypse Now*: "The Horror! The Horror!" It is an appropriate transfer, as the movie and Conrad's novel both explored the depth of darkness inherent in the human heart.

As the day unfolded, and the deaths mounted (I had hoped--prayed--that the perpetrators had flown empty planes), the full weight of the atrocity came to bear. The first grape customers were picking in the vineyard as I went between the fields and the television coverage. Probably for me the most poignant moment of the whole tragedy came as a small group of firefighters aligned in formation. There were about twenty-five of them in five rows of five each. They proceeded to march in formation in the direction of the first tower. The twenty-fifth fireman fell behind slightly, perhaps hesitant understandably in the face of what unknown danger. He then hop-skipped back into formation, regaining stride and step with his company. I thought of Doug Waters, a fireman.

Minutes later the tower came down. There was no way that noble troop survived. In the few seconds that scene was recorded, a story was told far more majestic than in any film or novel: the courage, hesitation, final resolve--perhaps knowing that they were going to their deaths. God Bless America. God Bless Americans like that. God Bless men like that anywhere.

To the people of New York, please know that from over three thousand miles away, you had the heart of a nation. To those who perished, our prayers and soulful compassion. And when the idiot who masterminded it crowed that Americans were afraid to travel, I answered with a sweet refrain heretofore reserved for selective service clerks who made similar attempts at restricting travel: "Bullshit!" I said. And I booked a ticket to go there.

My intentions were to contribute, in some small way, a gram of goodwill, to support in an equally small financial way the firemen, police officers, and Red Cross volunteers. I did not go to ground zero. I went just as one man, and to offer a single-finger salute to those who had committed one of mankind's worst atrocities.

I had never been to New York, had even avoided the place. It hadn't treated my manuscript submissions well; it had perhaps taken part in the plagiarism of one of them. I went expecting to find a Joan Crawford, but instead found a Grace Kelly. I fell in love with the city. The buildings with the "New Yorker" and "Scribner's" signs were shrines. Walking out into the street around some scaffolding, I came to the front of the building to discover: "Oh look, it's Carnegie Hall!" My answer to the question, "How do you get to Carnegie Hall?" is "Through the gutter." I took ten steps down the street to note, "Oh look, and there's the Russian Tea Room."

I had gone on the Internet before leaving and had written an invitation to local residents, generated in goodwill, to dinner or lunch or a show. It was not intended as a call to romance, but as one from a gentleman extended to a lady in a city that had just been raped. Interestingly, the response was positive and I had two dates a day, and all but one was with a Libra: the scales, justice; one man's attempt at leveling things a bit. There were two personal successes. I made one lifelong friend. And I had the meal of a lifetime in Little Italy, at Il Cortille.

You can sense as you enter the place that you are in for a treat if you like Italian food. The small tables, not fancy, with white tablecloths; the waiters with white aprons; the aromas from the noisy kitchen; the crowded atmosphere are all clues. In spite of having a reservation, you are escorted to a platform/mezzanine bar above the main dining area to wait for a table to open up. It isn't a great inconvenience, but agony if you are hungry and anticipate the offerings (fighting the expectations to avoid disappointment).

It isn't a long wait, and the vastness of the menu renews the anticipation. I have been told by Italian friends that I dine more like an Italian than most Italians. (It's one of my most cherished compliments--there really aren't many other ones.) I explain to my date my theory about doggy-bagging. When the food is superb, I believe in ordering from the entire menu way more than will be consumed so that the greatest variety can be sampled; the remainder can be doggy-bagged to be enjoyed the next day as a memory refresher. We do this: shrimp so light and delicate that the analogy to consuming clouds is accurate; pumpkin risotto; eggplant; of course a Caesar salad with a Pinot Grigio. Then veal, pasta, tomato sauces, and cheeses with a Chianti. A second table has to be pushed alongside to hold the overflow. Two waiters were pressed into service to present the fare. The first one was from Italy and about to go home for his annual vacation. I say something to make him laugh and notice that neighboring diners are laughing, too: Life. Celebration of it. You can almost see a circle glowing with good spirit and enjoyment in the staff and other patrons. I knew that this was why I had come. One small effort of goodwill was confirmed when the manager in formal-wear black tie comes up as we are leaving. He is tall, for all the world a character from *The Godfather*. He says in a deep throaty baritone voice that rings with authority, "Mr. Jones, I want you to know, you will never have to wait for a table here again."

Mission accomplished.

Chapter 26

If you come to a fork in the road, take it.
--Yogi Berra

It is fitting that in 2002, the Year of the Horse, harvest would begin with a return of some home winemakers who also raise horses. It is ironic that this harvest would also be marked with another insect encounter. I had gone out to test the sugar in the grapes that were going to be harvested that day. It was a bright, hot day and I set a can of beer on the fence post (it takes a lot of beer to make wine, you know). Satisfied with a reading of just over 24 degrees Brix, I took a long hard drink only to discover--way too late--that it was also the favorite brew of a yellow jacket that had gone inside the can. It became firmly attached to the inside of my lower lip (yellow jackets bite, they don't sting) giving me the appearance of a Ubangi and a speech impediment that made it sound like I had several more than just the one beer.

The previous year, Frank Disanti had come walking across the yard with two orange Home Depot buckets with all of the enthusiasm of a first-time winemaker. He had never made wine before, and as a result I had my suspicions about what he intended to do with those buckets. I asked him about them and he confirmed that he intended to use them as fermenters. He is a chemist by education and profession and I had a hunch that with his Italian heritage (he only wanted Sangiovese) and meticulous lab technique that he had the potential of achieving a sound result. "Your wine is going to taste like orange buckets, Frank," I admonished. "Invest in some food-grade ones." We discussed the basics of making wine, emphasizing cleanliness and protection from air. Nothing complicated...the bare essentials...aspects that a professional chemist would take to like a duck to water.

Apparently he had taken the advice about the orange buckets to heart. He brought a bottle of his initial attempt that he had even taken the time to label. Still young, only a year old, it poured with a clarity and color that would garner any oenophile's admiration. There was a clear rim around the surface, bespeaking the youthfulness, and a nose that spelled out fruit, grapes, and a hint of cherry that made you impatient to taste it. There was no disappointment, only astonishment. A marvelous complexity of smooth texture, balanced tannin and acid, and more, more, more fruit...confirmation to the grape grower, also pride. "Frank, this is as good as any American Sangiovese I've ever tasted."

I had no problem with this pronouncement. It included my own attempt. I hadn't concentrated on the making, being so consumed with the growing. He had been, as predicted, meticulous in his care of the wine and it showed. We compared it to mine, which was not as smooth, but had enough character to not be poured down the sink.

A couple of weeks later, I tried another grape customer's Zin made from my grapes. He had used oak chips, which I consider an anathema. The oak chips are used when aging in glass or neutral containers to impart the flavor of the wood to wine. Wine traditionally gets its flavor from aging in barrels. Oak chips are a way for wine made in small amounts to get that oak flavor...if you want it. My preference is for wine to express the fruit that it is made from. Having lived in Greece, where they use pine resin to make their retsina, I had developed an aversion to wood flavoring in wine. I think that overly oaked wine can also be an abomination. This customer's Zin was not overly oaked however and there was plenty of fruit. The oak chips were forgivable. The wine was good, again better than mine, but not as good as some I had been given a month before.

I'd had some free time over the winter to finish the cabinets in the kitchen. I wanted stained glass doors on those above the sink but had been thwarted by the high cost. I got quotes for some simple patterns that seemed more in line for a replacement of the north rose window in the Cathedral of Notre Dame. I thought I was going to have to settle for plain glass when, through a series of happy coincidences, I was given the name of a woman in Paso Robles who did stained glass. Her last name should be a familiar one to the reader: Dusi. Kathy was the niece of Benito and the daughter of his brother, Dante, who also grew heritage-quality Zin.

Kathy was a bright light and life-enthusiastic and came up with a design that was more cost effective than some plain glass ones. These cabinet doors now adorn my kitchen. Kathy also made wine. Her studio was in the center of her father's vineyard. Her wine was equal in quality to her stained-glass work. I noted that she had aged hers in an oak barrel. A seed of a truth had been planted, or perhaps more accurately, a seed of a paradigm shift (reserving the right to change my mind). We traded a few bottles of our 2001 vintages.

If I had ever had a better Zin than the one Kathy made, her wine made me forget it. *Superb* would begin an apt description: the color, the nose, the texture, the flavor from first on the tongue to the memory of it on the palate. I felt humbled—like the memory of that batting sessions several decades before in college. But the wines I had offered in trade weren't complete strike outs. They weren't home-runs like hers, maybe, but not without their merit—bunt singles, maybe, to her grand-slam. I wasn't going to retire my pruning shears to the same closet that held my baseball glove. I just had to spend some time in the *farm* leagues. (When you have a metaphor working, you just gotta milk it. But this one does end here. I promise. Any more would digress into PUN-ishment.)

Later, at the Midstate Fair in Paso Robles, the credibility of my grapes would get a big boost. So would the confidence of the grape grower. The fair is certainly one of the premier events of the Central Coast. The mainstage entertainment attracts first line performances of eclectic diversity that has ranged from the late George Burnes to Bob Dylan in addition to the traditional rodeo or tractor pull. The exhibits have all of the trappings of an old-time fair. There is pie-baking and 4-H livestock, and one of my favorites: the paintings and drawings from local artists. Of course there is the wine competition. I found Kathy Dusi's entry almost immediately. I went into shock. It had won the silver medal. "Jeeze, what must have won the gold?" I wondered.

I soon found that entry. The winemaker was Michael Dusi, her brother. Oh would I like to have been a fly on the wall at their next family meal. Then I noticed the bronze medal winner. It was the oak-chipped one made from the grapes of the Volo Del Corvo vineyard.

In that discovery, I had noticed that the Sangiovese silver medal went to that Mr. Grapevine who had recommended the use of chemicals that I refused to use on my land. That kinda stung. But just to the right was the gold medal winner: Frank Disanti, the first-time wine maker, who made his wine from my first-year-in-production vines grown from those Mondavi cuttings. "There is a God," I muttered and the lady standing next to me took two sidesteps away from me.

The horse year had progressed with a tranquility that was the antithesis of the previous year. The grasshoppers, which usually don't repeat that sort of performance two years in a row, had been combated successfully by disking and using a miraculous antigrasshopper artillery known as Nolo Bait. The active ingredient is a single-celled microsporidium protozoan (*Nosema locustae*). This microscopic animal is impregnated in wheat bran and is broadcast as you would grass seed. It has absolutely no ill affect on anything but grasshoppers and crickets. You could probably put milk on it and have it for breakfast, though it is not recommended.

There was even some time to work on the house, to tile the porches, and begin landscaping. A lawn was planned and Doug Waters was called in to trench for the sprinkler system. The plan was that as soon as Doug cleared the trench, I would drop in the water and electric lines and he would then follow behind me, refilling the trenches with dirt. The driveway would be impassable for a couple of hours.

But then, there is that saying, that if you want to make God laugh, tell him your plans. I am quite sure that my experiences had earned a regularly scheduled time slot on Heaven's comedy channel. As Doug crisscrossed my front yard like a super mole, events were unfolding that were about to force me into the role of my most amused fan. I was about to be put into the position of playing God.

Chapter 27

If you live to be one hundred, you've got it made. Very few people die past that age.
--George Burns

When I came in for lunch, there was a message on my answering machine. I recognized the number on the caller ID as my mother's. The following day was Mother's Day. "She's probably calling to remind me," I thought.

But the voice on the machine wasn't my mother's. It was her housekeeper's. Mom had been taken to the hospital in an ambulance the previous evening. This was not the first time. During the past several years she had made several such trips. Endowed by her with a medical-care power of attorney, I'd had a host of conversations with her and her physicians about a leaking aorta. Mom had refused surgery against the advice of the doctors, and she also had outlived by several years their most optimistic prognosis. My role was to understand her condition, make sure she understood it, and then respect her decision.

We had discussed retirement living but she was independent and more than a bit ornery and I sympathized with her, knowing the active self-sufficient life she had led. I tried to put myself in her place. I wouldn't have wanted that for myself either. I wasn't going to insist upon it for her. She had several employees for assistance. In some way, I was giving back what she had given me: her life.

The housekeeper left the number of the hospital some four hundred miles south in Orange County. In a matter of seconds, I was connected to her private room and her assigned nurse. I identified myself and inquired about her status. She was not conscious and was on a respirator and IV solutions. As a former army medic, I had a pretty good idea of the scene. She was "resting comfortably."

I telephoned my sister, her only other living relative. I advised her that I had been assigned a medical power of attorney. And particularly about one clause of that power: *No life support.*

One of my earliest memories was of being instructed to obey my parents. The words "acknowledge what I say" were gospel. The instructions spelled out in the power were authored by Mom during a time of lucidity that preceded the decline of the past two years. It had been difficult for her, and she had been, true to her nature, difficult right back. Finally, I was the one only remaining of her children and stepchildren who still maintained communication with her. Probably the decision I had to make would have been easier for any of the others. I could have sold the rights on eBay.

I verified with her personal nurse that she was indeed on life support...that she was not responding, was unconscious. I told the nurse of my instructions. She warned of the consequences. I asked whether there weren't times when patients survived on their own. "Yes, there are," came the reply.

I didn't see that I had any choice. Thanking the nurse, I said we would let my mother rest over night with the support, but if there wasn't any improvement...I didn't finish the thought.

The next day, I called when the same nurse was back on duty. There had been no change, good or bad, in Mom's condition. I asked that the telephone be placed by my mother's ear and for the nurse to watch for any response. "Mom, this is Ken. If you can hear me, please move your finger." The nurse said there was no response. I repeated the request, louder and sterner...a command. No Response.

"Mom, this is no way to spend Mother's Day," I was trying to be cavalier. Humor had always been the method of choice when dealing with my mother. It had been so when I was four; it was true at fifty-four. But the stone silence was like a cold slap in the face of reality and of the gravity of what was taking place. I could remember her words: "Acknowledge what I say." My parents had drilled us on obedience.

"I want to thank you for my life...for the introduction to music and art and literature," I said. Flashback snapshots of her at the piano, taking me to a traveling exhibit of Van Gogh, reading to me as a boy with fried-egg sandwiches when it was raining at Rincon. "Godspeed," I stated.

I apologized to the nurse for having to do it but asked that the respirator be removed. And for several hours my mother did continue to breathe on her own. But she did not improve, and on Mother's Day, 2003, she went out on her own--her way.

The front yard at my house was crisscrossed with open trenches and unassembled sprinkler pipe as I postponed the completion of the project with Doug Waters. In preparation for the temporary disruption of the project, I laid three rows of pipe across my driveway to stop any visitors from driving into one of the trenches and began to pack for the trip to Southern California.

Chapter 28

Life, a Four-Letter Sentence

I did not begin when I was born, nor when I was conceived. I have been growing, developing, through incalculable myriads of millenniums.

--Jack London

I adopted the theory of reincarnation when I was 26. Genius is experience. Some seem to think that it is a gift or talent, but it is the fruit of long experience in many lives
--Henry Ford

I guess, with all of the life lessons being delivered in the vineyard, that a little balance from another source was in order. When my stepfather died nearly a decade before, the event launched some serious soul searching and raised a chain of questions. He had confided years before, suffering from Parkinson's, that he was ready to go. The last years for him were suffered and death was a relief. So why feel so bad when it finally came? I had a ton to be grateful for with what he had given: the great laugh sessions, the instructions, the example he set. There just wouldn't be any more new ones.

It seemed to me that the first order of sentiment should begin with gratitude. Feeling bad because you don't get any more was almost ungracious. Since death has been the result of every life so far, to assume that it was a negative event would imply that life is tragic. I didn't want to accept that.

Now bear with me here, as it might sound a little-too-much-in-the-sun California flaky. It may sound like a little peel is coming off the orange (we used to have oranges in

California), and before moving to the country, it might have seemed so to me, too. I was intellectually interested in the subject of reincarnation. I am not talking alien abduction here. It does not involve shaving heads and bothering people in busy airport terminals, though you can find some support for reincarnation in most of the world's great religions--even the Bible. Remarkably, it gained some personal substantiation, several years before, from an unexpected source: my Mom.

The intellectual interest in reincarnation evolved from dream research. On several occasions I had dreamed very creative passages that were incorporated into my writing. This is not uncommon. Songwriter Paul McCartney dreamed the lyrics to *Yesterday*. I wanted to tap into that source of creativity more if I could. The problem was, I didn't remember many of my dreams. I bought books in an effort to do better, and they helped some. But I wondered if hypnosis might not offer some assistance. I wasn't even sure if I was a candidate for hypnosis. But I was going to find out.

Through a chain of medical and psychology professional references, I was put in contact with a psychologist who was also a renowned author. I was not seeking a Las Vegas lounge entertainer, I wanted a scientific professional. Dr. Bonnie Greenwell filled that bill.

The first session produced profound results and led to two more over a span of several years. Dr. Greenwell was extremely skilled as she guided me to a state of extreme relaxation. I wasn't even sure that I was hypnotized. The outside sounds of the conscious world could still be heard (birds singing, automobile traffic), but what unfolded was like a very creative writing session. I had hoped to find a prior life as Alexander the Great or Napoleon, but apparently I was a hobo. The account began where I had spent the night in a railroad tunnel. The time seemed to be in the late 1800s. A life unfolded in what I believed was the Rocky Mountains because of the terrain and the first characters I encountered. They were a father and his son, hunting. They were wearing flat, wide-brimmed hats and I took them to be Mormons.

Later in the session, silver was discovered in the small community where I settled and prospered. There was a riotous scene at the train station, where the celebrants were taking down the station sign and putting up a new one that read in spoof, "Yukon."

Later in the session, I mentioned a rumor that the president of the United States might be coming to celebrate the state's admission to the Union. In preparation for it, I had purchased a bolt of lime-green velvet that a smooth-talking traveling salesman assured me was the latest thing in Eastern (U.S.) fashion. (Just the thing that a grape grower might do in a previous life.) Bonnie astutely inquired who the president was. In retrospect what unfolded was charming. First, a feeling of exasperation at such a dumb question. Everyone knew who the president was. It was Grover Cleveland (stupid).

I did not recount the actual visit, and have not been able to confirm subsequently that Cleveland ever visited any of the Rocky Mountain states. However, a quick Internet search shows that the state of Utah was admitted during Cleveland's second term, in 1896, the same year as the Klondike strike in the Yukon Territory. I can also tell you that prior to that session, I had so little knowledge of Grover Cleveland that I could not have told you where in history he stood. I could not have told you if he had been president before or after Abraham Lincoln.

My other two regression hypnosis sessions also had kernels that lent support to their veracity. In one, I was a Jewish prisoner on a Spanish ship during the time of the Inquisition. The ship had run aground and all the crew had evacuated, leaving me to regain my freedom if I could make it ashore through the icy waters. The sensation of cold was so real that Dr. Greenwell had to retrieve a blanket to help relieve the almost uncontrollable shivering. I do not ever remember having been so cold. I wasn't remembering an experience, I was reliving it.

In the third experiment, I appeared as a Mayan. I was in thick foliage, barefoot, with mud oozing up between my toes. I thought how strange it was that I was barefoot, as the Mayans wore sandals. I should mention that I have a voracious interest in Mayan history. I have visited sites in Mexico, Belize, and Guatemala. I have had profound experiences of insight during those visits while fully awake, sober, and lucid that would be too much of a digression to go into here.

As in the two previous sessions, an adventurous story unfolded. I didn't think much more about being barefoot in the mud until months later when my mother, about a year before she died, not knowing about the hypnosis sessions but knowing of my interest in Mayan history, sent me an article she clipped from a magazine. She rarely sent me magazine clippings of any kind, and I was surprised that she had even remembered my interest in the Mayans, so sending this one was a little out of the ordinary. It was about a current archeological project in Central America and Mexico. Scientists were trying to establish the connections between the various Mayan cities. The Mayans had some excellent roads between some of the cities. But many had been overgrown and deteriorated. The scientists explained that the mud was so thick that they found it easier going by taking off their boots...and going barefooted.

The point here is that there was something very confirming about the experience...events that seemed so real and that could be tied to historical credibility. This is enough for me to be able to accept what otherwise might be viewed as a universal tragedy; instead, it is one that is very spiritual and majestic...also very mysterious. Death happens...it is inevitable...but I no longer subscribe to the idea that it is a misfortune. We come kicking and screaming into this world as we relinquish the security of the known comfort of the womb (of which we later have no conscious memory). My take is that we get comfortable here and are dragged into whatever comes next, going out kicking and screaming (I probably will) only to have something unfold at the next phase that is equally fulfilling and challenging. Whatever, I just hope they make wine there.

I had received some insight into one of Ben Franklin's two certainties--death--and would soon learn more than I ever wanted to know about the other-- taxes.

Chapter 29

A countryman between two lawyers is like a
fish between two cats.
--Benjamin Franklin
The only way you can beat the lawyers is to
die with nothing.
--Will Rogers
You don't pay taxes--they take taxes.
--Chris Rock

When my mother's attorney announced that she had named me as one of two trustees, I had no idea what that entailed. He told me that I would need to hire an attorney...and an accountant. He also informed me that he could not be that attorney because of potential conflicts of interest, having been Mom's councilor. What I soon found out is that dying is one of the most complex taxable transactions ever invented. Originally, the death tax was invented to pay for the expenses of World War I. One thing to note: once the inventors of a tax invent one, it is guaranteed a long shelf life. World War I was over nearly a century ago. Most of the inventors of taxes are, or were at one time, attorneys. Making taxes complicated benefits attorneys who are employed to wade through the complications.

I have to smile when I recall the symbolism associated with the Crow: the law and the messenger of truth. It does seem an oxymoron. But in one way or another, I had been involved in both activities since moving here a decade ago. The writing by choice and the law by intrusion: a divorce, the possible plagiarism that had gleaned $9 million for another writer, and now, estate tax law. Not that I needed another hobby right then. Since starting the vineyards, finish work on the house such as cabinetry and wall painting had been put on the back shelf. I had finally gotten around to doing some landscaping when Mom died. I already had three full-time jobs. I had been handed a fourth.

The first attorney (one recommended by my mother's) told me that the process would take about one year. His fee was three hundred dollars per hour. He instructed me that the responsibility of the trustee was to identify and protect the assets of the estate. My new fourth job became the primary one because of the urgency of such matters as paying Mom's outstanding bills and changing the locks on her house so that it could be secured and inventoried for assets.

Meanwhile, the attorney fees began to mount immediately, nearly ten thousand dollars for writing a few e-mails and reading the will and trust documents and talking to me on the telephone a few times. Recently there has been a great deal of activity in government to liberalize the death tax. It is far better today than it was several years ago when my mother died, though still an atrocity just by the complexity of the whole mess. Ordinary income tax filing is bad enough. Filing estate taxes compared to filing income taxes is like piloting the space shuttle compared to a ride at Disneyland.

Harvest was timed with the search for the second attorney, as conflicts of interest developed--his and ours. I sold a few hundred pounds of grapes, and made nearly the legal limit of home wine—one hundred gallons. The new attorney returned most of my phone calls promptly, which was an improvement, leaving me to pour through the boxes and files that I had moved from Mom's house and that now filled most of the first floor of mine. I was looking for evidence of assets.

I devised a schedule where I would get up at two a.m. and work until six going through the files and boxes of papers. I had to have these ready by February, the nine-month filing deadline (what an unfortunate choice of words). The plan was that working early in the morning would then free me up to work the daylight hours in the vineyard. The gophers were especially active this year and I just didn't have time to wage war against them like I would have liked. As a consequence, I realized that I would need some assistance in the vineyard.

The vines needed trimming and cuttings had to be collected and rooted to replace the ones the gophers got. There was at least the hope of being nearly through with preparing the estate tax. The time had just about run on the first attorney's prediction that it would take a year or a year and a half. But--and it would not be unfair to say, a very big *but*--the second attorney announced that we were going to have to file for an extension...that we weren't ready. I told him that I was ready, which at least established where the unreadiness lay. "When did you think we would be filing?" I asked. "March, April at the latest," he (rep)lied.

I really wanted to hire a part-time college student to help in the vineyard. Actually, the prospect of finding a Scandinavian one whose other job was as a lingerie model seemed attractive. But those hopes were dashed when I found out that I would be paying more for insurance, workman's comp, and paperwork, than the employee would receive.

The labor contractors had served me well in the past. The savings of using contract labor is huge when you only are talking about one or two workers. For the most part the guys that worked for me were good workers. The amount of work in a day that several can accomplish is staggering when you are used to seeing your solo daily progress. There were a few bad apples, and they were culled from the barrel. The problem was that so were the good ones. I always made it a point to tell the contractor when the quality of work was good and slowly began to realize that I never saw them again as the contractor sent them to other workplaces.

I also told the workers when they did good work, and at the end of the week I paid them a few extra dollars in cash. I enjoyed working alongside of them. The thirty-some year's difference in age set up some friendly competitions, and I was glad for the ability to make them laugh in their language. Occasionally they even offered to share their lunches. Let me tell you that those guys eat well. I am still not sure whether it is homemade or from small *tiendas*, probably both. In turn, I often gave them packages of meat if I had just shot a wild pig.

Several times I would get a pig when they were working and I would give them the whole thing. Later, when the weather turned hot, I provided sports drinks for them in the afternoon in addition to keeping their water jug full and cold. Having worked in jobs that I would regard as beneath fieldwork as a student, I have evolved an attitude that dictates that you do whatever job there is to the best of your ability. Within reason, of course: a toilet bowl doesn't have to be as clean as a surgical table (both jobs that I have done, in fact, both jobs that I did in the army for far less pay than these workers got). The result is that I have developed respect more for the quality of the work than the prestige of the job. Respect: R-E-S-P-E-C-T...which is more than I had for the legal profession.

March came and went, so did April, then May, June, and July. I felt ambivalent about the message from the attorney on my answering machine. I had come up to the house to collect a couple more flats of rooted plants while the contract workers waited in the field. The promised March filing was a forgotten hope, four months delinquent by my timetable, though still in compliance with the IRS extension. "We" were running up on the deadline of the extension to file, I was informed. My experience in editing and deadlines perhaps added to the exasperation. He had promised this would be completed fifteen weeks ago.

In fact the deadline was only two days away. "Marvelous," I thought, and I conveyed this sentiment to the attorney: that I would have to let the workers go early, that it was not the most convenient time to be driving sixty miles. I think I made some suggestion that he might want to relocate his office off of such a busy street where the ambulance traffic wouldn't be so distracting.

It wasn't with the greatest affection that I entered the attorney's office that day. Oh, he had offered to send out his paralegal to gain my signature, at one hundred dollars an hour and two hours' travel time. I went without showering. I listened as he explained what the phone-book-size document was that he laid in front of me. I raised a question about one section. There was a silent pause. He had made a mistake, he admitted. It was in our favor. "Go ahead and sign it," he instructed me. "The IRS probably won't catch it anyway."

The line above where I was to place my signature read, "To the best of my knowledge, all of the above is correct." My legal advisor was advising me to sign, knowing that all of the above wasn't true? I remembered a scene thirty years before, where an attorney said that if I would sign the document before me stating that I was against all war, I would not have to go into the army. My answer was the same.

"I can't sign this," I said. The attorney's eyes grew wide, then his brows wrinkled. He looked down at the document as if he had never seen it before. "It is going to take a couple of hours to change," he pouted. His first thought was that I would come back tomorrow. I told him I wasn't coming back. I would wait. I had come directly from the fields and probably didn't need to tell anyone that. I hadn't eaten yet that day, so I told him I would do that and come back...*that day*.

Across the street from the multistory office building that housed several other attorneys as well as a major stock brokerage, a tractor was tilling rows in the dark, fertile soil made famous by Steinbeck. Several blocks away, I found one of those hole-in-the-wall *taquerías* and dived into a plate of enchiladas, beans, and rice that could set the world right if there was World War III going on outside. Almost a year and a half after my mother's death, the papers would finally be signed. Another nine months or so (I was told) and the IRS would approve them. *Ha!*

I was glad for the diversion of working the vineyard. It was an anchorage in a world seemingly gone crazy: Taxes upon taxes and when your intention is to pay what is due (but not more), you have to hire what amounts to a new family member who is schooled in how to fill out the forms so confusing that a mere layman could never wade through them. It didn't help that at the time (unlike World War I, which had only cost twenty-two billion dollars) we were involved in a new conflict in Iraq and Afghanistan whose price tag would be in the trillions. I had thought we had finished all of that kind of business with the war in Vietnam. But the drive home from the lawyer's would lend some balance in a way that even the vineyards couldn't.

Chapter 30

Action speaks louder than words but not nearly as often.
--Mark Twain

Driving home from Salinas in the evening, traffic is heavy but moves at the speed limit (or just a tad above) even at the height of rush hour. The brake lights didn't initially portend anything out of the ordinary. It is common along this section of Highway 101, what the realtors have dubbed California's Central Coast, for an agricultural vehicle to momentarily disrupt the usually orderly flow of traffic. The realtors also call this particular part of the Central Coast *Steinbeck Country*, and the vehicles associated with the growing, harvesting, and marketing of lettuce, broccoli, and onions get concessions here. Usually just a serial flash of brake lights until whatever it is can scoot out of traffic. But the rate of slowing was faster than usual--something more than a tractor towing a trailer full of irrigation pipe.

The accident must have occurred only moments before. A cloud of dust still rose over the two vehicles on the side of the road. One was overturned, the other, apparently once a van, had its left side sliced away and was up on two wheels, leaning against a pair of trees. The driver hung out from the shoulder harness unconscious, probably not alive, a young child on the ground screaming was being attended to by one of the first to stop. Already there were at least three uninvolved cars stopped behind the wreck. Two more had pulled over into the central divider and two more going in the opposite direction had also stopped. A broad-shouldered plumbing contractor (identified by the sign on his still-open truck cab door) strode across two lanes of traffic and the center island, not pausing to shut that door of his truck. A fashionably dressed lady, probably from the luxury sedan, knelt by the child. A couple from the SUV were struggling with the passenger door of the overturned vehicle...total strangers, going to the aid of those in need.

I reached for my cell phone as I pulled over, just past the collision. I wondered if anyone had called for help, but before I could even dial 9, a California Highway Patrol car, lights flashing, raced up from the south. And before I could put the phone down, an ambulance appeared from the same direction. Deciding that more qualified assistance was at hand, I proceeded on my way home...thankful for not having been in the accident, sorry for those who were, and grateful for a society that had within it the kind of people who had stopped and an organization that had professional emergency assistance there within minutes. It was kinda nice to know that you had neighbors like that.

I couldn't help but think, though, that they deserved a better government. And this same sentiment would arise again soon among a group assembled in my dining room, as I had an announcement to make.

Chapter 31

*You should go to other people's funerals,
or else they won't go to yours.*

--Yogi Berra

People in casual clothes appropriate for the transition from summer to winter--jeans and flannel or sweatshirts with faded alma mater logos--gathered around the table. To celebrate the harvest, I gave a small dinner party for a couple of my grape customers. Actually, I only had a couple of customers. A majority of the vines were still too young to produce. I had shot a small boar for the occasion and made sausage to serve as an appetizer to precede the ribs and ham that turned on the charcoal spit. The guests each brought their wine made from my grapes. With the late, bright sun streaming through the west-facing windows, bowls full of slaw, sourdough rolls, artichokes, and twice-baked potatoes it could have been a Norman Rockwell painting.

Wild pork is leaner than farm raised. The meat is darker, less sweet. The ham--not cured--needs some applesauce or chutney to liven it up, and then goes well with the Sangiovese. One of the attendees was the first-time winemaker who won the gold two years previously. It still sparkled. A nose promised an initial taste of fruit--grapes and plums--then good tannins and balanced acidity, and a clean finish that leaves the palate ready to accept the next bite.

The ribs, slathered with spices and sauces that would make sawdust palatable, go well with the bigger Zinfandel, which, with the cherry and touch of cinnamon, can stand up better to the sweet barbecue sauce, having a little more work to do to cleanse the palate. The finish isn't quite as clean with a little more tannin, balanced quite nicely by the acidity.

There was one discovery that I would make (not an original discovery, but a discovery of my own). It had to do with aging. The wine that won that gold medal was still as fine, if not finer, as when it won that honor. But my wine, which had been racked less (I try not to overdo the wine making) and had more tannin, had now aged another two years. The tannins were smoother and if it wasn't as good as the gold-medal winner, it was a close second.

And here is a wine-making lesson that can extend to life in general: the value of conditions improving over time. How many occasions do you worry over a problem, sometimes agonize over it (like dealing with the IRS), only to look back in retrospect at how well it was resolved and how futile the worry was. Worry does have the productive aspect of inciting action, but when whatever action can be taken has been executed (one of those unfortunate choices of words), then any more worry is a waste of time.

But then there are some of us that just have to go out and find something else to worry about. And in that vein, I am constantly guilty. Tranquility just is not going to be part of my destiny. I made the announcement at that dinner that I was going to become a winery.

Chapter 32

*A learned blockhead is a greater blockhead
than an ignorant one.*

--Ben Franklin

Be always sure you're right, then go ahead

--Davy Crockett

You can't say that I hadn't been warned. You can't say that I wasn't aware of the warnings, and had spent several months agonizing over them. I was learned, but in April 2005, I bit the bullet. I was smitten beyond redemption. The passion for the work and the end result of wine making had taken a close second seat to writing. I just liked doing it. I decided to begin the dreaded process of becoming a bonded winery--dreaded because of the unknown bureaucratic and economic morass. It was well founded. Let no dread go unfulfilled.

I tried to disguise this foolhardiness with a costume of reason: I had sold grapes and had offered de-stemming and crushing as a free service...half the work toward the final product (it is really less than half, but I was disguising foolhardiness here). Instead of selling the grapes at fifty cents a pound, or about twenty-five dollars a case, I thought I might be able to follow through and make ten times that for the end result.

When I was seven, Davy Crockett, through the Walt Disney television biography, asserted an influence personally as well as universally that had few parallels. I can still remember the saying, "Be sure you're right, then go ahead."

This was well over a half-century ago. It is certainly a credit to Fess Parker, who became an American Icon as Davy, that such a positive influence can persevere for over fifty years. I seem to recall that the saying was preceded by, "Before you act, think twice." That saying certainly describes the process I had been going through about trying to start a winery, having thought more than twice. It didn't hurt any that Mr. Parker in real life went on to start a premier winery in the Santa Barbara area. It seemed that all of my heroes were doing that.

I was certainly ignorant of what it would entail to become a winery. I would find that there are three levels of government involved: local (Monterey County), state (Kaliforn-ee-uh as it has come to be pronounced by Austrian-born governors), and federal. Within each there are several agencies that have to be appeased. The experience in publishing and house building and vineyard planting was good preparation: establishing the order and priority of what to do first. Before you can put on the roof, you need walls, and before the walls, you need a foundation. Before you go to press, you have to have type set, before the type is set, the articles have to be written and edited.

Of highest priority was getting the federal status of a bonded winery. It is illegal, otherwise, to make more than one hundred gallons of wine per individual per year. If you do, you are a bootlegger and the revenuers will be after you through the briar patch. And the penalties for violations are not small.

In my early journalism days, I had the opportunity to visit a white-lightning still in rural Georgia. The bootlegger was reluctant to take me there, but was bullied into it by a friend of mine, to whom he owed money. For all the world it was a scene out of a Faulkner novel. Cruising the rural country road where you might have expected the Dukes of Hazard to show up around the next corner, and parking about a mile away from the still, we wrestled with a barbed-wire fence that tore hell out of my trousers. Stumbling along in my city clothes not designed for the trek, we paused every few minutes just to listen for any other presence. The closer we got to the still, the larger the beads of sweat on the bootlegger's forehead. He had already been caught once and a second conviction meant prison for him. I had no idea what it might have meant for me, but the outlaw aspect was delicious--for the day.

My friend pointed to a sack high up in the branches of a tree: "Creosote," he advised. "To help mask the odor."

The actual still was a bit of a disappointment. It was just a pot on a propane burner, a coil to condense the spirits that boiled off, and a few glass jugs to collect the distillate. The bootlegger replaced the nearly full catch jug with an empty one and we left almost immediately, heading in the direction away from the car. We angled back toward the road, depositing the full jug in the brush. The three of us strolled back up the road to the car, then drove back to the jug which was hastily placed in the trunk of the car. The poor bootlegger was sweating bullets. We took him home, waiting as he brought us a small pickle jar full of his most recent vintage.

This was no barrel-select Bordeaux. While the liquid was clear and resembled vodka, it burned going down and had a slight flavor of the grain--corn--that sent a shudder through the upper torso as the digestive system complained. When I declined a second sample, my friend wheeled into a little clapboard country store and bought a six-pack of Fresca and a couple of paper cups.

I have never been a great fan of Fresca and the white lightning did nothing to improve it. But my friend was hell-bent on introducing me to the fineries of rural southern life, which also included chaw. There was that brief glowing moment of the authentic American South before the nausea set in. It was a vengeful, unrelenting hangover that lasted well into the next day and remains vivid several decades later.

Equally indelible is the memory of terror on the face of the moonshiner as he guided a stranger to what was a potential prison sentence had I been an undercover revenuer or committed some blunder that would attract the attention of one.

The reason for the laws that govern alcoholic beverage manufacture is twofold. With distilled spirits there is the health issue. Impurities have commonly caused blindness and can even make the product lethal...risks that don't carry over into wine making. The primary rationale for the laws, however, is revenue--hence the term revenuer for those who enforce the tax laws.

The process of making wine legally begins with the county use permit. Living rurally there is no city business license here, but the county fathers have to be reassured that what you are doing isn't going to adversely affect the general welfare. They don't want you operating jackhammers in a hospital zone or dumping garbage in the community's drinking water. There are good reasons for having some control over the activities of those who have displayed a lack of sanity by pursuing such endeavors in the first place.

Several months earlier, I had made an initial inquiry about the process with the county and met one of the most affable, courteous people since Doug Waters. Lynne H. Mounday, whose title was Planning and Building Services manager, was coming out to my area anyway and to gain some familiarity with my project offered to drop in. I conducted him on a tour of what I might be doing and where I might be doing it. The end result was that my plan was doable--no hospitals or reservoirs nearby...the nearest neighbor was a quarter mile away. He actually made the idea sound sane.

What I gleaned from that meeting was that normally the use permit process took about four months. What I inferred, and quite incorrectly, was that since my project required no new construction, was so removed from impacting anyone, and was so small in scope that it might be accomplished quicker. Timely acquisition of the permit was essential, as the state and federal permits depended on it, and you had to be a bonded winery (federal) before you could pick one grape. That federal permit took only about four weeks (they get the tax revenue). Normally harvest starts in September, which was cutting it close, but experience as a magazine editor told me it could be done.

The division of the Monterey County Planning and Building Inspection Department that handled winery permits was temporarily housed on what had been Fort Ord, where I had taken basic training in the late 1960s. Fort Ord was decommissioned in the '90s and as time wounds all heels, I took great delight in revisiting my old penitentiary. I was still around and it wasn't.

The planning office was of more recent construction than the decaying barracks that surrounded it. Double glass doors and linoleum tile floors, a stainless steel drinking fountain and sturdy counter were undoubtedly all according to code. Secretaries scurried, men in work boots with a dozen rolls of building plans pored over an unrolled one on the counter across from a casually dressed clerk in a plaid short-sleeved shirt.

There was an attractive young lady with great legs at a sort of school desk with a sign taped to it that read something to the effect of "Start Here." The sign ended just above the knees, but I knew what it really meant, so I started there. "I would like to get a winery permit," I explained. What I envisioned was a sheet of paper that said, "I want to start a winery." I would fill it out with my name and address, and in a few weeks (sixteen at the max) it would be sent back to me with a red "approved" stamp on it....Uh-uh.

"Do you have your packet?" she asked. The voice went with the nice legs.

Packet? There was a deafening silence as reality collided with expectations. I was pretty sure that she wasn't asking a personal question. Since I didn't know what a packet was, she was also well assured that I didn't have one. I didn't know whether I should be hurt, offended, or grateful. "Please take a seat; someone will be with you in a minute."

The seats were two rows of hard-plastic-covered, chromed-tubing-armed chairs like those in barbershops lined up along the walls opposite the barber chairs. The Monterey

County Planning and Building Inspection Department did not furnish magazines, however. This left me little to do but worry about what a "packet" entailed. Also ponder the strange distortion of time and space that I had just entered.

A Monterey County Planning and Building Inspection "minute" has no relationship to any measured by a standard timepiece...at least any of those in use today. My watch and the clock on the wall marked off several of their minutes, about twenty, before a clerk appeared with a gray paper folder. It opened to two pockets stuffed with forms, instructions on filling out forms, and instructions on reading the other instructions.

For almost a complete rotation of the timepiece on the wall, I thumbed through the folder, bewildered. The first line of the Instructions told me I was going to be coming back. Lynne Mounday, who had been out to my house and had assured me of the acceptability of my project, happened by and stopped to chat. He helped with several of my initial questions.

"What's a Coastal Development Permit?" I inquired. It turned out that I didn't need one...unless the next earthquake put me closer to the ocean. However, in spite of the fact that I planned no new construction, a great many of the questions would be about the physical operation: photographs, elevations, plot plans, site plans, and existing building plans. I don't think the D-Day invasion was as well *planned*. There was no way I would have been able to fill it out by close of business. The clincher: not only did I have to fill all of this out, I would have to fill it out and make ten copies. I suspected that the people who designed these forms also held stock in local photocopying services.

I had gone into the office expecting to file an application to be a winery. I went out with enough homework to stifle a PhD candidate. I closed my partially completed packet. As I left my steel-armed seat, I reflected on how I really preferred the barbershop reading material. There was absolutely nothing in the center of the folder, let alone any photographs.

In all fairness, I could understand the reasons for many of the questions and information required. Pollution and safety are good things to be concerned about. And it is good to see that there is some guard for these in our society. And I was able to make another appointment in a week to submit my "packet" and ten copies of it. The cost was $6,375.68: Six thousand dollars for permission to make wine. If I hadn't thought the idea of becoming a winery was crazy, I did now. Being a quarter of a mile from the nearest neighbor and forty times that distance from the nearest waterway, you might have thought it wouldn't be so rigorous. But I have to tell you, the hoops they have set up for you to jump through, you would think you were going to make hand grenades for Osama bin Laden. I have a theory that our laws are enforced to keep those who obey them in a perpetual prison of proving that they are obeying them, rather than preventing disobeyers from breaking them.

The one personal exception might be speeding. Something that the recipient of my six thousand dollars would never be found guilty of I would soon discover. I could not be entirely sure, but as I left the planning and building office, I thought I saw, dozing in one of those chrome-armed chairs (I could be wrong about this)...but he looked an awful lot like Jimmy Hoffa...right next to a chair occupied by an ancient old lady in an aviatrix costume.

Chapter 33

Angels and Demands

You can take the future even if you fail
I believe in angels
--Lyrics from *I Have a Dream* by Abba

Spring is probably the most beautiful time of year anywhere. It certainly is at the Volo Del Corvo. Probably the climate is what sold me on being here. To the east is the Salinas Valley, the setting for *East of Eden*. Eden is an apt description of here. It is also a lot like Tuscany. Winter here is short lived--January through March--and it's summer almost the rest of the year. Spring is like summer in most other parts of the world.

There is a race to trim the vines before bud break. The new growth that will spawn the fruit is a light tan. This has to be trimmed back to rule-of-thumb three buds. Any longer than that and you will get two bunches of fruit on the branch, any less and there is a chance of not getting any at all. The bureaucratic forms and the attendant dent in the bank account are forgotten as vine trimming, gopher getting, and irrigation mending take over.

Apparently I wasn't the only one who had forgotten about the application. Somewhere along the way, I received a letter stating that a name had been assigned to oversee whatever it was that they do with the packets. I certainly didn't know what that was. I thought of it like some mystical conveyor belt that goes into a tube and in four months comes out the other end with some sort of stamp on it. For all I knew the ten copies were distributed among ten paper airplane makers who set about madly folding them into highly imaginative gliders and launched them from atop the Steinbeck Center.

For all the world, reality wasn't much less productive. After three months, I thought I had better check on the progress. It turned out there hadn't been any. After leaving several messages with the name on the form, I contacted Lynne Mounday. It turns out that the county had bestowed upon itself a new building. The move to these facilities had not accelerated the processing of my application. As a matter of fact, nothing at all had been done. When a voice that belonged to the form name actually appeared in my telephone, it asked if I planned to make wine *this* year. I realized that I was in trouble.

One unanswered question in my mind was, Did it take four months to process the application marked from the date they started doing anything or was it a case of doing nothing for three and a half months, then doing something for half an hour before giving me my permit? Maybe the manufacture of wine permits is like the product being permitted. It has to age until exactly the right time, then be plucked from the in-basket and...and maybe I had been too naïve about the process. Maybe I should have started inquiring about the progress months ago. Maybe...

I knew that the county permit was the basis of all further licenses--the state and federal ones. The federal one was the critical one. It is illegal to even pinch a grape before you are federally licensed (bonded) if you intend to sell the wine made from it. According to their website, that required a little over a month. There was less than two months before harvest. The state restrictions were a little more accommodating. You could make all the wine you wanted, you just couldn't sell it without a license. Or at least that's how I understood it.

A telephone call to the TTB ensued. They used to be called the ATF (Alcohol, Tobacco and Firearms). I am not sure why they changed the name. Probably to avoid confusion with state agencies that are also called ATF. Nobody had taken up the name TTB. It stands for Alcohol and Tobacco Tax and Trade Bureau. The *firearms* part has been taken out of it, presumably in order to make room for the bureaucracy part.

A blur of telephone calls followed and a procession of referrals to those more in the know about getting the permit to make wine. Along the way, I must have gotten some wires crossed with an ecclesiastical telephone network, for eventually I was connected to an angel. Her name was Julie, and she listened--listened--as I explained my problem. I told her that I understood that I had to have my business permit with the county before getting the federal one. I explained that I had applied for it three months before and still didn't have it. I understood that the normal time required (a courtesy estimate) was forty-five days. And that it was required before even picking a single grape. And finally my problem was that in about that time my grapes were going to be ripe.

"Do you have an application number for your county permit?" the angel asked.

"Yes," my heart leapt...there was a feeling of a great weight being lifted from it. For the first time in weeks, I was able to actually answer a question affirmatively. The clouds parted, a ray of sunshine streaked down in glorious golden illumination. Cue the choir, seraphim, and cherubs. With that number I could begin the process of getting my federal permit.

I was also able to get started on the state one. The state permit was not as much a sticking point as the federal. You could start the wine without it, you just couldn't sell it. Much of the material needed for the county could be copied over for use in the other two. The map requirements were about the same, and because of my rural location this wasn't a stumbling point. They just wanted to know where it was that I would be doing this, to make sure I wasn't dumping skins and stems over a neighbor's fence. And also they wanted to know where it would be done on the property so that an inspection could be made without going into my attic.

And, as if they were feeling neglected like an aging film star whose bloom had come and gone, I started getting requests from different county agencies. My permit had been transferred to a new planner--another angel, by the name of Paula--who furnished me with a list of agencies from water quality to the fire department that had to be satisfied. The stairway functioned as a file system for the process, three rows across, eight steps down, with a completion pile (that was becoming bigger) at the top for each: county, state, and federal. The federal had highest priority and so that row was near the center of the stairs (a path being left for ascent and descent), followed by county and state. The hot items were on the bottom step.

When I called the state agency, I was informed that I would need an appointment. Here was the archetype of all efficient bureaucratic workers, caught up in earning a living by enforcing, implementing, and completing the requirements--bearing the brunt--of those who had created the bureaucracy in the first place: the lawyers and politicians.

One thing that you have to understand is that the people who work in these agencies are not the ones responsible for them, and by and large, if given the opportunity, they are expediters. They are there to assist you through the process. With few exceptions they were courteous, proficient, knowledgeable, and deserving of gratitude. At times, they could be angels. The state agent was a unique case. She had been doing her job for over two decades and was on the verge of retirement; she let you know right off that this tune was going to be played according to her meter. She only processed three applications a day, by appointment, and you had better be ready for your appointment, or you would go back to the end of the line and wait a couple more weeks.

In retrospect, I regard the memory with affection, though at the time, it seemed a little arbitrary--arrogant even (an angel in a demon's disguise)--that she only handled three applications a day...and that it would take about two weeks to get such an appointment.

Being ready meant having all of the forms completed. I had to post large signs--one at the gate and one in my front window--announcing the intent to sell and distribute alcoholic beverages. To protect the sign from the rain, the one at the gate had to be laminated. A local print and copy house did that, too. Being ready also meant that I had to be fingerprinted. This is done at the sheriff's office. It is just like in the movies, all ten digits. I was now "in the system." And by the date of my appointment, I was ready.

The diminutive wisp of a figure could have been a live incarnation of the grannyesque owner of Tweety Bird and Sylvester from the cartoons. Yet she had the aura (and probably the authority) of an NFL defensive lineman. She had an assemblage of tools from highlighters to post-its and paper clips that she wielded like a neurosurgeon. Places where I was to sign were X-ed. Information that I had to supply--blanks on forms--were highlighted. Completed forms were clipped and turned face down. I had misunderstood one of the forms and had not supplied the material needed. But this was apparently within the realm of acceptability (a moment of dread about having to schedule a second appointment) and she produced a nifty little tube that White-Outed my incorrect answers, leaving a clean platform for the correct information.

A couple of times, her attention was distracted by questions from less-experienced staffers. Their questions answered, she returned to the process at hand until finally all of the forms were in the face-down stack: Completed. There were a couple of other milestones, a waiting period and an inspection of my premises. Oh, and I had to go to the State Board of Equalization (the ones who collect the tax) and get a retail permit as well as a winery registration. See what I mean about completing one process only to have two more spring up?

The state and federal requirements were cakewalks compared to the county use permit. New fires kept springing up just as an old one was extinguished. An apt choice of metaphors, as I would find out shortly. For the single largest official obstacle to becoming a winery would be posed by the fire department. Unofficially, however, the dogs were inventing impediments of their own with an almost diabolical creativity.

Chapter 34

In The Heat of the Bite

When a dog runs at you, whistle for him.
--Henry David Thoreau

At about the time that the county wasn't doing anything with my use permit, the dogs took it upon themselves to go into exploring mode. Of the 160 acres that make up the ranch, about thirty are fairly heavily covered in brush, scrub oak, a few pines, and several large white oaks. The habitat supports three species of rabbit, as well as squirrels, skunks, raccoons, wild boar, and occasionally bobcats, deer, and coyotes. It is a wonderland for Labrador retrievers. Hugo, the troublemaker even as a pup, was usually the instigator of such forays as an adult. If ever there has been evidence of a rogue by nature he would be it. Being confined to the dog run, he became like a kid on Easter, having had his fill of religion.

The first time that the three got out, coyotes had been roaming, hunting the area in packs. You could hear their frenzy of yips and howls that becomes more frantic as they surround their prey and then silence. As darkness fell, and my roaming idiots had not returned, I grew more concerned. I had searched several times during the day, driving to high ground at several locations on the ranch, also the surrounding main roads. But to no avail. Sometimes I might find them coming out of a neighbor's corral. More often, I would spot them crossing the hill opposite the house. Still on my property, I would bound out in my Forester and retrieve them. Policy was never to punish: either on their return or collection. I didn't want to make either a bad thing. Perhaps a lesson learned from a father's belt.

As a result both occasions became festive events: a homecoming to be celebrated, or if they were apprehended, "OK, you got us this time"--all in good fun. Discovering their absence, I would go to the upstairs balcony and glass the 270-degree panorama as part of the ritual. On one occasion, they showed the height of the sport. Their having been gone for several hours and my having completed several searches, I put down my binoculars, softly cussing them for being gone and causing me the anxiety, when out of the corner of my eye I caught some movement directly below me. It was a bright, hot sunny day and it took a few seconds to realize that there were teeth shining in the shadows of the aboveground pool directly below me...three mouthsful. I swear to heaven, they were laughing...children having been discovered in a game of hide-and-seek. Darned dogs.

On this occasion, however, it was late spring and the weather was not so hot to drive them home--perfect, in fact, for long distance roaming. They weren't coming home until they were hungry...or had satisfied the hunger of the coyotes. Evening came, and when I heard a band hunting in the north part of the ranch, I even drove out in the dark, fearful of what I might find.

The yelp-dogs are clever. While they are usually not bigger than a Lab, they are wild hardened and also hunt in packs. They have been known to send out a female in heat to attract a family pet into an ambush. Hearing them hunt that evening, in areas where I suspected my dogs were, I thought the worst and feared finding the mauled carcass of Virginia, the smallest and most vulnerable, in the headlights as I searched.

I returned home without seeing any sign of dogs or predator, hoping that the boys might have survived, anticipating some severe wounds if they had. But at about midnight, I was in the kitchen and just in case I checked the back door and was startled by the three stooges, thirst ravaged and hungry. Not a single wound. For all the world, they were still partying and came in like a band of rowdy friends. You would have almost expected that they would have brought a six-pack and a couple of bags of chips.

Ginnie was twelve now, eighty-four in dog years. But she would still go into heat. And as my application was aging with the county, she selected that as an appropriate time to express her femininity. The mudroom, which is connected to (and extends) the dogs' normal "family room," has to be partitioned off with a half sheet of plywood, then the door to the laundry room is opened to extend her majesty's suite. The boys still have the doggy door contact to the run, but Ginnie has to be accorded regular promenades from the back door. The area out of there is not fenced and her forays have to be monitored so that she doesn't wander. As she was invited back in, she was informed that she was being a royal pain in the ass, which thoroughly delighted her. She had a wonderful half bark that she developed as an enthusiastic response when I addressed her. "Yabbabba abba," she sort of snorted, half-barked.

Normally she was pretty good about staying close to the house when she was on her own, but not always, and when I left her unattended for longer than was prudent, I was as mad at myself as I was with her when she went missing. Often, I would call her and she would come scampering happily along the back of the orchard fence. But on a rare occasion she wouldn't respond. In an hour or two, or three or four as was the case this time, she would return. She was filthy and full of slobber and burrs and small oak leaves. As the coyotes were still hanging around, I accused her of having illicit relations with them, using the shortest single-word description that profane English affords. "Yabba abba abba," she replied, not in denial, tail wagging happily.

Apparently the Monterey County Planning and Building Inspection Department, Ginnie, and the IRS are all on the same lunar calendar, for it was at this time that Planning presented me with their to-do list. And, as if synchronized, the IRS finally deemed it time to request some additional information concerning my mother's estate (two years after her death and a year after receiving the return).

This put a real crimp on the replanting and the annual one acre of new planting. But, as I was ushering Queen Ginnie back to her throne room, I noticed a large swollen area above her right hind knee. At the center of the swelling, there was a small, insect sting-like wound. It oozed slightly, and as I wiped it with alcohol, it appeared that there might be two punctures. I had killed a baby rattler just the day before near the woodpile. That coupled with the fact that both the boys had been bitten in the past and I had initially dismissed both of those as yellow jacket bites led to all else being put on hold. We were going to the vet's. Of course it was Sunday and the nearest clinic was an additional twenty miles further than the sixty for the regular vet, who is closed on Sunday.

Except for a slight limp, Ginnie was in great sprits...."Yababba abba abba" she chattered as she jumped into the back of the Subaru. A rooster tail of dust rose behind us to the gate and all posted speed limits were exceeded by precisely fifteen miles per hour, hoping that if stopped it would be by a dog-loving patrolman.

The trip was reminiscent of the one with my ex-wife during her first labor. Except this time I didn't take any wrong off-ramps, and in just over an hour we covered ground that would normally have taken half again as long.

Chapter 35

And Now the Fire Department?

... skewered through and through with office-pens, and bound hand and foot with red tape.
--Charles Dickens

As we waited for the vet to see Ginnie, I poured over the county to-do list, trying to salvage some productivity out of the day. Most of the items were within the realm of reason, save one...from the fire department. In constructing my home, they weren't my favorite voice: recall the smoke detector that goes off every time I light my pipe in my office, the sewing room that had to have its name changed from third bedroom because the windows weren't large enough to accommodate a fat firefighter with breathing apparatus (I guess fat firefighters can get through sewing room windows better than bedroom ones), the self-closing steel door to the attached garage that makes carrying in two armloads of groceries at the same time impossible. I had no antipathy for the profession, however. To repeat, it isn't the ones responsible for the laws who have to administer and enforce them.

My respect for the profession goes back to the coaching youth sports days when half of the other teams were coached by either law enforcement officers or firefighters (the fact that my teams usually beat them only enhanced the affection). One of my objectives in going back to New York right after 911 was to donate a small amount to the police and firefighters. Those guys anywhere put their lives on the line daily. They are good men, by and large, good fathers, and it isn't their fault they can't coach (just kidding). Nor are these laws their fault. They are, in the end, the ones who have to oversee them.

Some of the requirements were minor inconveniences. There are size standards for street-address-number signs. I needed a new sign anyway. The old one, approved when I had built the house, was made of wood and had split. The new one had to be made of fireproof material (presumably not wood) and had to be visible by traffic coming from both directions. The road dead ends about a quarter of a mile above me. There are no firehouses up there, and for a firefighter to come from that direction, he would have to pass through several locked gates and/or off-road it for several miles. I hoped that good visibility from the one direction would be sufficient. There was a requirement for a fire-detection system, and the installation of twenty thousand gallons of water storage.

Later, when talking to the local fire official, an officer at the nearest fire station, I realized that all he was doing was following the requirements of his job as administrator and enforcer of the laws he was sworn to uphold. I was curious about the increased water requirements, since I wasn't doing anything to increase the fire hazard. "Wine can put out fires," I told him.

"It doesn't matter what you make or do," he explained. "You are now commercial."

"Commercial?" What it came down to was that if you were going to attempt an enterprise where you might be making a couple of bucks, the county was going to see to it that you jumped through a few hoops first. None of which were bigger than the water storage requirement one.

Standing fifteen feet from my front porch is a twelve by thirty-three–foot, aboveground pool. There are twenty-two thousand gallons of water in it. Monterey County does not count water in swimming pools as fire-fighting water. It is perfectly good fire-fighting water and when I discussed this with Doug Waters, the assistant fire chief at the fort, he told me that a pump capable of using lake and pond and swimming pool water is standard equipment on all fire trucks. In neighboring San Luis Obispo County, in fact, not only are swimming pools considered acceptable vessels for fire-fighting water, they are accepted as the source for water used in fire-fighting sprinkler systems.

As it turns out, the problem was not with the fire-fighting quality of the water, but with the quality of the swimming pool owners. In Monterey County, swimming pool owners don't keep water in their swimming pools. Or at least that was how it was explained to me by the firefighter assigned to my case...the same one who explained to me about the *commercial* status change. "We have found that too many people build swimming pools to satisfy the fire requirements, and then leave them empty," I was informed.

That reasoning was ridiculous (at least in my case). In the five years since I've installed it, that pool has never been empty. My water tanks, which I also use for irrigation, are empty several times daily. As we were in August when the average high temperature is in the nineties and frequently in the triple digits, it was difficult to imagine anyone with an empty swimming pool.

In retrospect, I realize that the laws are not made by the firefighters charged with their enforcement. Nor is the official position that they are forced to distribute as the rationale for the laws of their creation. My reaction was precipitated by the prospect of having to add ten thousand dollars worth of tanks and spend several days in the construction when the required water was fifteen feet away from my house already. I felt badly that brave good men who place their lives in jeopardy daily in the interest of public safety are placed in such a position.

As remarkable as the laws and their enforcement were, there was a totally satisfactory solution that would eventually be reached. Meanwhile, the veterinarian could not tell for sure whether Ginnie had been bitten. The swelling hadn't gotten any worse. If it was a bite, it might have been that not much venom had been successfully injected. The vet gave us some antibiotics in case of any secondary infection and instructions to apply hot compresses three times a day. An additional indignity was imposed on her: one of those cones where the small end ties around the neck and the big end extends out like a megaphone gone wrong--the RCA dog with a master that doesn't like rap music--to keep her from licking the site.

The dictionary defines paranoia as an extreme, irrational feeling of persecution. I wonder if anyone who has ever started a winery hasn't fallen into this sensation. As it seems like every government agency but the INS was coming down on me about something, it was soon to extend to agents other than those from the government and even to the dogs. Thank heaven that progress was being made and there was the work to balance those feelings. As Yogi Berra said, "If the world was perfect, then it wouldn't be." The world was sure getting there. Yeah, Kafka all over again.

Chapter 36

Beware the hobby that eats.

--Benjamin Franklin

Virginia was so good natured that the cone barely slowed her down. She might have been making a passive-aggressive statement as she crashed into my shins with it, though. At morning, midday, and night we had our hot-compress sessions, which she regarded as spa treatments. We had a routine where she would lay on the uninjured side and I would sit down on the floor of the bathroom with a bucket of hot water and several towels, changing them often. I told her what a pain in the ass she was being, and that would start the perennial wagging tail, thumping on the unfinished floor, almost falling asleep: Cleopatra in ecstasy.

She didn't seem to be in any pain and put up with that cone. I also thought it would keep her close to home. And when I left her unattended too long one morning and she didn't come back right away, I started looking for her, concerned that she would get that cone hung up and become trapped in the brush. The concern was compounded by the fact that she didn't bark. She had the capacity to, and only on two occasions do I remember her using it: once when she was tending her litter and someone came to one of the garage windows and looked in, and once when someone came to retrieve the last of the pups.

In my search, I did find the cone. She had managed to free herself of that at least. And several hours later, she came padding around the garage happily almost as if to say,

"Wassup?" I probably should have noticed then that she wasn't exactly acting herself, but was so busy with the grapes and the gripes that I was just relieved that she appeared to be fine.

Harvest had now started. The various agencies had been sufficiently satisfied to make this legal. And a couple of workers had been hired to assist with this, the first, commercial harvest (starting to sound like the fire marshal). I had been delinquent in emptying one of the fermentation tanks, so as the workers brought in grapes, I had to make room. At that time I only had six fermentation tanks of three hundred liter capacity each. The tank that needed emptying contained some Zin that I had aged for a year and a half in an almost neutral barrel. When I had transferred it to the stainless, I thought it had oxidized and anticipated throwing it out. Remember my aversion to oak? Well, when I pumped it out of the barrel into the stainless tank, I thought it had been confirmed.

But when I sampled the stuff that had been aging another several months, I was taken with the aroma of fresh fruit and cinnamon like no wine I had made heretofore. I was reminded of Kathy Dusi's bottle of wine, which she had traded for some of my earlier efforts (an unfair trade). But here was something that would have made comparison more equitable. It was a little heavy on the tannins, but I really do like it that way. Oak was no longer an anathema.

Although most wine made in America (until recently) has seen some oak, in my initial wine-making efforts I had scorned the use of it. "Wine should taste like fruit, not furniture," articulated a bias formed from having lived in Greece where they resinate their wine with pine. It took months to get used to that, and no time at all, once having returned home, to get used to its absence. But I had also always reserved the right to alter my opinion. Not about pine, but oak. That reservation awakened with the wine Kathy Dusi had made. It should be acknowledged here that there is a trend away from oak, especially with white wines, among American winemakers.

By now, the reader probably has noticed a penchant for experimenting. I mixed portions of the oaked with the nonoaked, then bottled offerings of all three. The results gave me one of the best educations about the merits (and demerits) of oak aging that I could have asked for. There was no disputing that the aroma of the oaked wine was superior in a nondining (tasting room) environment. And that carried through to the flavor, though the other two weren't exactly vinegar, just more subtle on the nose. I had to admit, if I were standing at the counter in a tasting room, the prettiest wine was the heaviest in oak. Since the barrel used was neutral (reconditioned and consequently not as flavorful as a new one), the oak was not overwhelming.

The real test then came when food was introduced into the tasting. With highly flavored barbecued ribs, for example, the oaked was superior. A sip of wine, that meat just jumped with flavor. It wasn't hurt by the other two, just better with wood. But with a less powerful food, such as cheese, the oak overpowered, and depending on the person (there is no right or wrong in wine, it is a personal experience) one or the other was preferable.

It became a hit at dinner parties to bring all three when asked to bring some of my wine (winemakers find themselves invited to more parties). Though it might not have been as popular with the hostess, who had to wash triple the glasses afterward. Guests toting three glasses each are soon swarming around the buffet, nibbling and sipping from one or another. Delightfully, preferences were never unanimous (there is no right or…well, you know).

What was universal was that each had a preference for one with one dish, and another with a different food…wine enhancing food, food enhancing wine.

So now, instead of throwing it out, I had to bottle about twelve cases. Note to self: You don't want to be bottling during harvest. You have enough to do just to keep up with the grapes as they come in. I was up until two getting that tank ready and bottling the best wine, by far, that I had ever made. But by six the next day, the tank was ready to receive the next day's picking. And as if there hadn't already been enough distractions, the boys--Hugo and Sartre--had escaped their run. It was probably the bad example set the previous day by Virginia. But then she was setting another bad example, presenting me with a seemingly perfectly detailed relief map of Greenland in diarrhea.

Had I been less occupied with other activities, I might have noticed that she had been setting a lot of bad examples lately. Normally obedient (at least on the second command), she seemed to be asserting a bit of independence.

The bad example that she had set for "the boys" was duplicated on their return as well, in the continents of North and South America in the same stuff, then Europe, Africa, and Asia. And that was just the first days. My guess was that a wild pig had died in the brush nearby and the meat had spoiled. My only hope was that the condition would improve before they ran out of continents. There were eight other planets.

In retrospect, I will always look back at her assertion of independence with affection, although at the time it seemed like a cynical cosmic joke. Harvest was in full bore, and a date had been set for the public meeting that would mark the official establishment of the winery. There was, in spite of the amateur cartographers, light at the end of the tunnel. I did not know then of the tunnel that loomed just around the corner.

Chapter 37

In a fight between you and the world,
back the world.

--Franz Kafka

Three weeks into harvest, I was looking for a place to park near the new Monterey County Courthouse (which I had helped furnish). I was late. There are several parking lots in the vicinity, all reserved for the employees. I found a place in front of three trash cans on a residential street. The trash hadn't been collected, and I didn't have time to consider the impact of my placing my car there. I was glad for the years of long-distance running, though the loafers didn't offer the support I would have liked. I retraced the route to the impressive new courthouse.

The chamber entry is very much like a theater. Instead of a stage or curtain at the front, there were two tiers of desks, not all occupied, that formed a front-open crescent of officials (not unlike a giant open-mouthed Pac-Man coming at the rest of the auditorium). Each had a microphone. At the center of the crescent, there was a podium also with a microphone facing the crescent (the dot about to be consumed by the Pac-Man). I am not sure what a tribunal is, but I thought that if this was a movie, it would be appropriate staging for the Inquisition. The audience side was not full either. There was someone at the podium addressing the crescent. The microphones made my late entry slightly less of an intrusion than entering a church in the middle of a sermon. My concern was that I had missed my appointed time.

Still out of breath, I found Paula (the new planner, who had gotten everything accomplished in just a couple of weeks that had been totally not done for three months). With minimal conversation she handed me a several-page document. The first page was a schedule of the day and mine was the last item. As it turned out I was two hours early. As harvest was in full session, I wished that I had known that. I could have spent the additional two hours picking grapes instead of attending hearings about property lines and development zonings that had absolutely no pertinence to my life.

Still, I was relieved to not be late, and of even greater relief was the time afforded to visit the men's room. Nerves, coffee, an hour drive, and a half-mile sprint, you know. It was an opportunity to see how my six thousand dollars had been spent. The chrome and tile were well maintained and I returned to the auditorium somewhat reassured and relieved.

The seats in the audience section were not as luxurious as the leather, high-backed ones of the crescent. But they were comfortable enough and I settled in to review the pages that I had just been presented. There were about twenty pages now to the document that the planner had prepared. I had seen most of it in one form or another. The requirements of the various agencies were noted as having been met, with the exception, of course, of the fire department. And here was the most pleasant surprise I had experienced in months. Oh, the fire requirements were there all right...everything from street sign to twenty thousand gallons of non–swimming-pool water. What had been added was the activation milestones associated with those requirements.

Months before, Lynne Mounday had recommended that if I ever planned to build any new buildings that it should be noted as a second phase on my use permit. It would save having to go through the whole process all over again. He had been out--had taken the time--to personally assess the scope of my project. I really had no immediate plans for putting up any new buildings--heck, I still had finish work on the one started a decade before: my house. But should I decide that I wanted to expand, the way would be paved.

By having the second phase, it gave those imposed with the responsibility of enforcing the laws and regulations some flexibility in that enforcement. I was a cottage operation, with no employees, no tasting room, and no increase of fire hazard. The water tanks, road paving, alarm system were all attached to various stages of the second phase--if and when there was one.

American ingenuity is given its due in technology, but on that early fall morning I was introduced to it in government bureaucracy. If and when I began the building process of a separate structure, I had been saved from doing the use permit process all over again. But more importantly, I had been saved the expense of overkill regulations with which I might otherwise have been compelled to comply. All of them tied to milestones in the new construction.

In a nutshell, as I sat there with documents spread out on the seats on both sides of me, I realized that I was done. In a matter of minutes, I would officially become a winery. And when it came my turn to take the podium, I did so with a great sense of relief and gratitude, which I expressed to the tribunal in front of me, particularly to Lynne and to the planner who had brought everything to completion.

Then the mischievous side kicked in; as I never like to let an audience go to waste, I saw the opportunity to get a laugh. I mentioned my plans for this book, subtitled, "How Not to Start a Winery." And I acknowledged that several chapters would go to emphasize that the paperwork should be started far more in advance of the first harvest than I had done. There was mild laughter, but when I produced a copy of *Waldo*, and announced that it would be available for sale outside, immediately following these proceedings, the room rang with laughter. The mirth was a fitting end and just one more way to repay the courtesy I eventually received.

I did not sell any books that day. I couldn't help but smile, though, as I made my way back to the car. But if there is one thing I have learned, you don't rest on your laurels. The grapes were getting riper. The sun was at noon-high. It was hot. Just enough time to get in a little shopping for provisions (I was out of beer) before heading home to harvest for a few hours in the cooler evening.

Actually, almost everything I had learned in the experiences of the last decade was about to be put to a test: "You may not be able to control the events in your life, but you can control your response to them." Even the worst experience can be the precursor of something good that wouldn't have come any other way.

Chapter 38

It ain't the heat, it's the humility.
--Yogi Berra

During harvest, even in the late afternoon and on into the evening, it can be hot in the vineyard. At first, I thought it was just a result of the stress of the morning, racing to the hearing, procuring my permit, and then racing back to work. I felt a little off. Perhaps the heat made me dizzy, but as I plucked fruit, whatever it was, it was getting worse.

There was a flu going around and the recent treks into the city, being fingerprinted, laminating signs that would announce my intent to sell alcoholic beverages, filing my fictitious business name and arranging for its publication in the newspaper had all conspired to see that strain was successfully transmitted to one more host.

This was one guest that I couldn't feel hospitable toward. Picking grapes, swinging fifty-pound baskets around in the heat, is hard work...glorious work when you are feeling well, but a special kind of heaven when the vine rows swirl when you stand up too fast.

That evening, the harvest tucked away for the next day's crush, I went to feed the dogs. As I let Ginnie out to "stretch" she kinda stumbled, seemed a little off-balance. Sympathy pains for the way I felt? The thought was charming, and considering how I felt, I was not entirely sure that I hadn't imagined it. It was just a brief moment and she came back in and seemed to eat with her customary vigor. The boys inhaled their meals. But the next day, she was a little lethargic, and ate indifferently. I was concerned, but not overly. But when she refused breakfast on the following day and seemed content just to lie in the corner, the concern was more serious. It was a Sunday, of course--the vet was closed, so I called the emergency clinic and described her symptoms.

One thought occurred to me, in fact if you Google the title of this book you can read about it. "The wrath of grapes" is a malady dogs suffer, thought to be brought on from consuming grapes or raisins. They are the very symptoms that Ginnie had: mild vomiting (not out of the ordinary), lethargy, lack of appetite (a real rarity). It is treatable but can be fatal as a result of kidney failure if not attended to in a timely manner.

I didn't want to wait for the vet to open on Monday, so I swept out the back of the Subaru and went in to collect the white dog. Her tail wagged as I called her, but she refused to get up. She couldn't stand. This was alarming--a memory of that dream about a pipe cleaner dog, trying to stand, being assured that it was alright not to--so eerie in retrospect, as just three days before she had been as lively as a pup. I swept her up in my arms the best that I could and laid her gently in the back of the car, her tail thumping softly on the house-moving pad.

It was a bright Sunday morning--perfect for picking grapes. I glanced at the sun as we drove down the drive, and it might have been my imagination, but I thought I detected stitches, as in the horsehide that had sent me to the ground almost forty years earlier. But this time there was no spin. It wasn't a breaking pitch and there was no bailing out. This pitch was no brushback. I was about to get beaned.

Chapter 39

Dog Is God Spelled Backwards

The last time that I saw her was in the emergency clinic. I didn't know it was the last time then, and in retrospect, it was better for me that I didn't know. I wonder now if she knew. The doctors and technicians had her on an IV. She was resting comfortably. I had all of the optimism in the world that she would recover and that I would be taking her home soon. I thought it was just the wrath-of-grapes thing and a few days on IV and she would be back on her feet.

We had been there before and she had always come through. I bent down and hugged her, buried my cheek in the soft familiar neck fur, told her that she was doing a good job (that she was getting well). She wagged her tail. One of the technicians moaned at the touching scene, at Ginnie's valor. And I left, courage bolstered by the wag, believing that I would return in a day or so to take her home, like we had done so many times before.

But not this time. It wasn't the grapes--Ginnie had cancer. Operable if she could get her strength back, but those efforts were failing. She was just getting weaker and weaker. On the third day, I made the decision to let her go. It was the saddest decision I have ever made. This time there were no written instructions about life support. The decision was mine alone.

I was thankful for the practice of always showing my appreciation to those close to me. For some reason, I have always been aware of mortality. I had long ago--when I made that to-do list that took me to Africa--made the decision to live my life like it was the last year, month, and day on earth. And to treat those close to me like it might be theirs...not an easy task, and admittedly I have failed at this on more occasions than I would like to admit. With my dogs, it was the frequent end-of-day session, before retiring, just telling them, "Thank you for being my dogs." I was glad that I had done that with Ginnie.

When I lose someone close or a pet, I try to identify their one greatest strength and assimilate it...an attempt at dealing with mortality with immortality. Something of them keeps on living. Ginnie's greatest strength was her happiness. With Virginia the identification was easy, a tail that wagged perennially. I remember when I took her home after her C-section the vet commented on her wagging tail. "It will be wagging long after she has left this earth," I replied, glad that I was taking her home. That was seven years ago. Now I was hell-bent to take on happiness...not easy as I buried her. And when the handle on the shovel broke, I just had to smile. "Ginnie," I muttered, "you are still being a pain in the ass." It was said with affection. When I would care for her in the past, applying compresses to abscesses, administering medication, taking her temperature, treating her wounds, I would end those sessions by telling her that she was doing a good job but that she was being a pain in the ass. She always took great delight in the pronouncement.

Several days later, I noticed on the calendar that I had made the decision to let Ginnie go on 10/3/05. By now the reader of this book knows the profound respect I hold for the spiritual implications of coincidences...and also my discipline to keep the experiences in balance. They are just road markers, assurances that you are going in the right direction, on the right path. The coincidence here was that on 5/10/03 I had given the instructions to have my mother removed from life support. I attribute the source of these events to the "Infinite Unknown," the term I use for God. While I try not to overemphasize them, I also don't dismiss these coincidences lightly. I can tell you, though, that I wonder what 5/3/10 might bring. I am planning to disconnect the telephone and spend the day in bed...or under it.

It was also through a series of coincidences that two books on the subject of "happiness" were recommended to me within a week of Virginia's death. These recommendations came from complete strangers, completely unknowing of my quest. The subject of happiness is not a simple one, and once you contemplate the complexity it becomes a labor of love. One of these books was so precisely on target that I will recommend it as one of the five most influential texts of my life. It is *The Art of Happiness* by the Dalai Lama.

The heart of the book is the concept of compassion. The premise: lack of compassion is an obstruction to happiness. The book offers a great deal more, but just that one grain of truth has been life altering. I have always approached relationships with the opposite sex and with children from a position of compassion. But I had never given much thought about extending it to those of my gender. No, this is not a coming out of the closet exposition. I am a died-in-the-wool confirmed heterosexual. In those relationships with the opposite sex, I have often stood back in wonder at the objects of my compassion. Fundamental are the questions: What is it that they want? What is it that they need? Often the answer is for me to go away. And I do that...sometimes reluctantly...sometimes fleeing with my dignity in shreds when the compassion isn't returned. Perhaps there are a lot of people of both genders that don't perceive that men need compassion, too.

I do know that when I am alone, I thrive without it. Without someone not giving it, it is easy to not miss it (wouldn't Yogi love that one?). Perhaps the ideal relationship is unconditional compassion...giving it without requiring it in return. And maybe that is the fundamental weakness of romantic relationships: of wanting compassion in return. And perhaps the definition of a good relationship is where compassion is free-flowing in each direction. And when it isn't, of knowing how to identify that it isn't free-flowing and being able to articulate it and correct the situation.

The epiphany that came as a result of reading that book happened at a pre–New Year's Eve party given by a friend. I am normally not much of a partygoer, but the person giving the party was a new acquaintance who had an interesting story, and there promised to be an eclectic assemblage. In general, the gathering was living up to my hopes. But in attendance was one individual who I took an almost immediate dislike to.

During several different conversations with others in attendance, he would come up and proceed to set himself up as an authority on whatever the subject at hand was...an arrogant authority. Readers of this book have probably deduced that I do not suffer arrogance very well. And during one conversation that he interrupted with his "knowledge" of computers, I unleashed my credentials as a computer programmer with fifteen years of experience that dated back to the days the company I worked for had a contract with IBM to provide software for their then-secret first PC.

The victory was a shallow one for me...the realization that I was being the arrogant one. I remembered a passage in *The Art of Happiness* in which the author described a similar situation. But he then had a paradigm shift and, as a result, ended up liking the other person. Remembering this I stopped for a minute and just looked at the arrogant one. If we had both had a little more to drink and he or I had taken it a little further, we might have both taken it outside.

Instead, I remembered the passage from the book and found myself asking the questions, "Who is this guy," "What does he want?" and "What can I give him?" I proceeded, perhaps rather clumsily, to ask these questions. "What do you do (for a living)?" "I am a trainer came the answer." He was a veteran of the war in Iraq. Then, and I am not sure how it happened to come out, he informed me that his father had died four days before. I was stunned. He was in intense pain...grief. And for the life of me I could not dislike him anymore. A great deal of the conversation that followed was a cathartic monologue on his part, and I was just grateful to be able to assist. And, on the drive home, I was grateful to a little yellow, almost white, dog. The gift that just keeps on giving. Tail still wagging.

Chapter 40

I don't believe people are looking for the meaning of life as much as they are looking for the experience of being alive.
--Joseph Campbell

All you need is ignorance and confidence and the success is sure.
--Mark Twain

Hard work is a great anesthesia. It was supplied by the ripening grapes and accelerated by the pickers not showing up. This might have been more disturbing if it wasn't for the serendipitous arrival of a message delivered through the "John Tesh Radio Show," which I often listen to as I work in the fields. It came as an affirmation: "I can do this." Mr. Tesh enthused about the power of just repeating this when faced with a challenge. I can attest to it. The calming affect is extraordinary. Standing alone in the vineyard, the loss of the pickers might have been disheartening but in fact their absence was welcome. I needed the solitude and the diversion of hard work. I could, in fact, *do this*. One bunch of grapes at a time.

I had hoped to get two hundred cases, but with over half of the grapes already picked, there were less than one hundred cases. I would lose some grapes to raisining if I finished solo, but there would be a savings offset by not having to pay any pickers. From dawn until noon, with a break for lunch, then until dark, there is the man-in-a-leaky-boat element to the work (the saying that no man works faster than one with a bucket in a leaky boat far from shore), but the mechanics of removing grapes from the vine was also a tonic. A knife rather than shears is the weapon of choice. Some of the smaller bunches could just be pinched off.

There is probably no lonelier sound on earth than a first bunch of grapes hitting an empty bucket. Then the bottom of the bucket is covered as more bunches are added. I am not fast at it. I have never been fast at anything that I can remember. Maybe driving. Driving too fast is the only crime I have ever been convicted of, and any nonconvictions have been victimless. Though, with all of the rules and regulations, I am sure I will happen into another transgression soon with one of the government agencies. As I am writing this, I have paid a fifty-dollar penalty for filing late a no-change/nothing-done report to the state.

The buckets I use for harvest hold about fifty pounds, about one case of wine. I pull two of them around in my little red wagon (the John Deere) and when it's full, get them to the shade, actually the entry room of my house, which is air-conditioned. Ten cases a day--ten buckets--is the best I have done. Fortunately, the grape varieties all have a few days' difference in ripening times, allowing me to work in rotation.

Not only do you have to pick the grapes, they have to be crushed and pressed, eventually finding their way to the basement as must. This means five steps up the front porch with a five-gallon bucket, sixteen steps down. The most I have processed in a day is a hundred gallons...three presses full...twenty-five round-trips. That comes out to 1,050 steps, travel of well over a mile. Fatigue becomes accumulative-- bone-tired exhaustion comes earlier each day.

I didn't get the two hundred cases. I was actually short by fifty. One hundred and fifty cases, about 375 gallons, is less than some wineries wash out of their empty tanks. But the quality of the juice showed promise. The acid needed little adjustment, the color and the flavor of the fruit was excellent.

There is a rhythm that builds and, with it, time to think. The Cab is the last to ripen. These were the plants featured in the television news piece about the grasshoppers. They were three years old then. Driving between the rows at that time, bugs spewed like gravel from the tires of a country boy's truck. The four-foot-long stems were left bare. The vines were now recovered and in full leaf; the fruit was plentiful, though small. I am not sure if the grasshoppers had anything to do with the diminished size or if the stark vineyard practices did it. No food, no pesticides, only water and the poor soil. But the flavor was undeniable. Even in the raw fruit, you could detect the Cabernet signature. There was also a hint of pepper, a bitter bite that was almost sexy. This would be blended with the last Sangiovese in the style of a Super Tuscan--a Super Tus-KEN. I had high hopes for this one, and on first racking these hopes were exceeded. I have a special affection for these vines, how they had survived and then thrived and now contributed to the catalogue with distinction.

A hundred and fifty cases does not represent a great financial success. If I got twenty dollars a bottle, deduct four dollars a bottle for the costs of bottles, corks, shipping, utilities, and taxes, that would come out to about $28,800. I have made that much in a month. Considering that I spend an average of eight hours a day (twelve to fourteen during harvest) in the vineyards, seven days a week, for about ten months per year, that comes out to about 2,400 hours or twelve dollars an hour. Not exactly the brightest endeavor...actually pretty dumb...in truth very dumb. But then I have done a lot of dumb things for no compensation at all.

There is something about swinging fifty-pound buckets of grapes around in 100 degree heat or pounding trellis stakes in hail. And then there is the special satisfaction of the end product, how it will enhance a grilled steak or bring out the flavor of a salmon fillet or add a glimmer to those eyes across the table in romantic candlelight. You know that warning that has to appear on alcoholic beverages concerning women who are pregnant? I am thinking of adding one of my own: how it can also contribute to that condition.

There have been a lot of lessons learned in this process (of starting the winery, not getting women pregnant). Life is surviving, and then hopefully thriving, as those grape vines have demonstrated--of meeting the conditions and handling it as best you can: *You may not be able to control the events in your life, but you can control your response to them.* As I think back on all of the experiences, from insects to bureaucrats (sometimes redundant), from tragic losses to humble gains, I can say that, at the very least, it does make one feel alive. At night, exhausted, you might not be so convinced, but in the morning, the pain of getting out of bed assures you it is so. I understand what George Burns meant when he said, "You know you're getting old when you stoop to tie your shoelaces and wonder what else you could do while you're down there."

One of the great benefits of harvest is that you sure do lose weight. I wonder if I could sell the idea that this is a spa treatment and charge great sums to young starlets slimming down for their next roles instead of paying farm workers? The possibility of a bevy of scantily clad *Eves* scurrying around in the vineyard is appealing, and it doesn't hurt to add it to that wish list.

I realize that past performance is not a guarantee of future results, but I do lose ten pounds during this time...and not too soon, as the holidays loom just ahead. You have to wonder if Thanksgiving was really invented by grape growers. It could not have been more appropriately located on the calendar. With the vines going into dormancy, the wine sealed away in tanks and barrels, there is little to do but to give thanks for that fact. And wouldn't you think that would be just one celebration that might go smoothly?

Chapter 41

Wine is constant proof that God loves us.
--Benjamin Franklin
(He said the same thing about beer.)

The leaves have turned to golds and browns on the vines. Since there hasn't been much rain, I am out irrigating the near-dormant vines almost as a courtesy. The weather is warm...Indian summer. And a quiet contentment sets in as the dogs--"the boys"--accompany me along on the inspection of the drip lines. It is not difficult to be thankful and to contemplate the ritual turkey dinner.

Now readers of this book might suspect that the path to this dinner might be fraught with an obstacle or two. First, it is delayed a day because I am still doing the preceding year's income tax a month late from the mid-October extension. One of two reasons for being late is that in mid-October the IRS review of my mother's estate had come to a final round of "negotiations." This after the Water Quality Control Board sent a multipage form to be completed...all during harvest. Harvest is busy enough without such distractions and I wrote the Water Quality Control Board a note stating this fact, that "such an inquiry during harvest was about as welcome as a telemarketer selling pogo sticks to a woman in child labor."

So Thanksgiving is delayed one day. It wouldn't diminish my thanks. And as a signal of good coming from adversity, Pier 1 has a sale on wineglasses. My dishwasher had been eating my old ones. The grocery-shopping foray would include a stop there. No self-respecting winery should be without wineglasses. All in all, the raid into town was going pretty smoothly. Except (you knew this was coming) there wasn't a pumpkin pie to be found...Thanksgiving without pumpkin pie?...unthinkable. The store had the cans to make one, but my office was full of receipts and calculator tapes and forms in chaos waiting to be organized during the bird roasting and I just didn't have the time or the experience to make one...so I selected a cherry one to partially fill the void. There is nothing wrong with cherry pies. It just didn't seem appropriate. Like chocolate sauce on asparagus.

By the time I got home it was too late to start the dinner, and some newfound discretion dictated that an additional day's delay was in order. Thanks was growing as was the appetite for roasted poultry. But as the purchases were put away, something was missing...two things actually. The package of bakery cookies that I had selected at the same time as the cherry pie wasn't here. Not a big deal and a check of the receipt showed that I hadn't paid for it. But then the stuffing mix, the package of seasoned, dried bread cubes, wasn't here either.

Now a Thanksgiving without pumpkin pie is almost inconceivable, but one without stuffing is just out of the question. A second check of the receipt showed that I hadn't been charged for that either. I could only guess that the items had been sent on to the person in front of me at checkout. Somewhere in San Luis Obispo County, a family had unwittingly purchased a package of fresh peanut butter cookies and a box of stuffing mix. A forty-mile trip into town to get replacements wasn't an attractive thought either.

For some reason, I began searching through the kitchen for a solution. I guess I thought that if I wished hard enough, a box of stuffing mix would appear. I don't make stuffing at any other time of year but miracle of miracles, tucked in behind the Bisquick and backup jars of mayonnaise and maple syrup, there was a box identical to the one that had been sent to the wrong home with the cookies. This one must have been left from the previous year (or the one before that). These boxes come with two sealed bags and one was still inside and sealed. It was only half the amount that the size of bird I had required, but what the heck, a half-stuffed bird was still something to be thankful for. And a check of the still-sealed contents revealed that the seal had worked...a little stale, but with onions and celery and chicken stock and a whole lotta butter, it was manageable. What was preposterous was that there was any bread cubes on hand at all. It was almost like I had willed it. Mind creating reality?

I was up early on Saturday morning. I pulled the bird from the refrigerator, and proceeded to wash and clean it, plucking off the pin feathers. Anticipation grew for the aroma of sage and fowl wafting through the house. I pulled the neck out of the bird, set it aside to be included with the gizzard, heart, and liver for the gravy. The right hand dived back into the cavity of the turkey. Inserted a little further, further still. My fingers protruded from where the head would have been. Empty. No giblets. Oh $#%&#! I retrieved the plastic bag that had contained the turkey. Boldly printed: Giblets Included. False advertising...$#%&# again.

No pumpkin pie, no stuffing, no giblets...absolutely untenable. I called the store...Albertson's. But before I lashed out at the voice on the other end, I remembered the book about happiness that had come into my library as a result of Ginnie's loss. Compassion had been the lesson. First, it wasn't the store's fault that the package was without giblets. So any animosity aimed at that voice would have been misdirected. I explained my plight and as I did so, it became funny. "A gibletless turkey"--it sounded like something my ex used to say about me. The voice laughed (always a good sign) and was very accommodating. They would give me a new bird. And no, I didn't need to bring the first one back. This generosity was contagious. I really didn't need two turkeys.

As it turned out, when I went back, the butchers were cutting some birds up and packaged the giblets from two, which were extended without charge. As I was waiting, I got a full box of stuffing mix and, luck of all luck, the bakery had a new supply of pumpkin pies. Life is good, and as I checked out of the store, I made the cashier laugh, too, with the story about it all. She left her station for a moment and returned with the manager's approval to offer the pie free too. The end of the story: the best, most succulent turkey, fully stuffed, with double giblet gravy and free pumpkin pie contrived to make the best Thanksgiving ever. It might have been my imagination, but I thought I could hear a white tail wagging.

Ending on a note of thanks would be an appropriate conclusion to this book...thankful for the experiences and satisfaction that have come out of the pursuit of a dream, in defeat and victory. I am most grateful for the former--if they don't kill you, they will make you stronger--and within them, you can find experiences to savor. Like the memory of that first pitch in college: the feel of solid contact with the meat of the bat, the ball sailing just past the bill of Thor's cap, digging up the turf behind second base. As for the victories: well, you learn not to expect them and to be grateful for them with humility. As I am writing this, I am preparing to bottle the first offering of the winery. Within each bottle is hope: Hope that the joy in making it is translated in the consumption (a sample tasting justifies the optimism). Hope that it doesn't go bad in the bottle, and that the fruit, tannins, and acid will enhance. Perhaps one of those bottles will be uncorked by a young man with a ring box in his coat pocket. Hope.

The hope is of course still tempered by that admonition about making small fortunes from bigger ones (and memories of life's corrective measures such as a father's belt). The hope also has its support. I have recounted how the first-time winemaker won the gold medal for wine made from my Sangiovese and how others have won medals for wine made from my grapes. Early on, I entered several of my own vintages. Because I made only a few bottles, I discontinued my submissions, not wanting to relinquish ten percent of my production for someone else to tell me it was good. I liked it, and that was enough. But I did receive encouragement from those early submissions...ribbons for my Sauvignon Blanc, Sangiovese, Zinfandel, and Barbera.

They weren't golds, or silvers. There wasn't anything metallic attached to any of them. They were honorable mentions...four of them.

Now, to my recollection, I had never been mentioned honorably for anything in my life, let alone four times.

There is hope for us all.

The author and his dogs and grapes live in southern
Monterey County, California.

He is currently working on a children's story, **Canary Road**,
and a novel, **Butterflies Bells and Mirrors**.

His first book, **Waldo, an all too true dog story**, is available
in hardback.

Logon to www.volodelcorvo.com for more information.